"*Mud, Rocks, Blazes* is beautifully written, intense, and exhilarating—a no holds barred, one-woman show. I held my breath often as Anderson faced seemingly impossible hurdles. You'll root for her every step of the way. Put this deeply personal and riveting book on your must-read list."

—**Barney Scout Mann, Triple Crowner and author of *Journeys North***

"Most of us may never know the physical and emotional toll that comes along with the challenge of setting an FKT [Fastest Known Time]. In this beautifully written book, Anish takes us along for the challenges and feeling of triumph that such an endeavor encompasses. You can't help but want to root for her up every hill and over every obstacle. Anish's story is an incredible reminder of the power of determination to accomplish great things."

—**Elsye "Chardonnay" Walker, first African American to complete the Triple Crown**

"The physical feat of setting an FKT is interesting in *Mud, Rocks, Blazes*, but even more fascinating is getting a perspective on the mental fortitude necessary to complete such a task. I couldn't put this book down!"

—**Sirena Rana, author of *Best Day Hikes on the Arizona National Scenic Trail***

"Many know Heather 'Anish' Anderson as a phenomenal athlete, yet, in this deeply personal account, she reveals powerful insight into her mental fortitude and gives us a glimpse into the heart it took to be the fastest known, self-supported AT thru-hiker. She overcomes mental and physical obstacles, and through it all, proves that her strength extends beyond her physicality."

—**Derick Lugo, author of *The Unlikely Thru-Hiker***

"Heather Anderson is one of the most impressive endurance athletes of our time. *Mud, Rocks, Blazes* beautifully captures the joy and misery of a wild, wonderful adventure. This is a story of perseverance, overcoming self-doubt, and believing that we can achieve anything if we want it enough."

—**Joe "Stringbean" McConaughy, record-setting thru-hiker**

"*Mud, Rocks, Blazes* brings to light not just the glorious moments on the trail, but reveals the depth of strength Heather Anderson needed to complete what most of us would call unimaginable."

—**Crystal Osborn, CEO of Hike Like a Woman**

MUD
ROCKS
BLAZES

LETTING GO ON THE
APPALACHIAN TRAIL

HEATHER "ANISH" ANDERSON

MOUNTAINEERS
BOOKS

MOUNTAINEERS BOOKS is dedicated to the exploration, preservation, and enjoyment of outdoor and wilderness areas.

1001 SW Klickitat Way, Suite 201, Seattle, WA 98134
800-553-4453, www.mountaineersbooks.org

Printed in the United States of America
Distributed in the United Kingdom by Cordee, www.cordee.co.uk

24 23 22 21   1 2 3 4 5

Copyeditor: Laura Lancaster
Design and layout: Melissa McFeeters
Cartographer: Martha Bostwick
All photographs by the author unless credited otherwise
Cover photograph: Will Swann

All descriptions, events, and dialogue described in this book are based on the author's personal memories, journals, and discussions with others. In a few instances names have been changed to protect privacy.

Library of Congress Cataloging-in-Publication Data
Names: Anderson, Heather Anish, author.
Title: Mud, rocks, blazes : letting go on the Appalachian Trail / Heather Anderson.
Description: Seattle, WA : Mountaineers Books, [2021] | Summary: "An account of a record-setting thru-hike of the Appalachian Trail"—Provided by publisher.
Identifiers: LCCN 2020033214 (print) | LCCN 2020033215 (ebook) |
ISBN 9781680513363 (paperback) | ISBN 9781680513370 (epub)
Subjects: LCSH: Hiking—Appalachian Trail. | Hikers—Appalachian Trail.
Classification: LCC GV199.42.A68 A52 2021 (print) | LCC GV199.42.A68 (ebook) |
DDC 796.510974—dc23
LC record available at https://lccn.loc.gov/2020033214
LC ebook record available at https://lccn.loc.gov/2020033215

Mountaineers Books titles may be purchased for corporate, educational, or other promotional sales, and our authors are available for a wide range of events. For information on special discounts or booking an author, contact our customer service at 800-553-4453 or mbooks@mountaineersbooks.org.

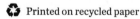 Printed on recycled paper

ISBN (paperback): 978-1-68051-336-3
ISBN (ebook): 978-1-68051-337-0

An independent nonprofit publisher since 1960

To my mother—
thank you for believing in me

CONTENTS

CANADA

Saint Lawrence R.

Lake
Ontario

Lake
Champlain

VERMONT

MAINE

Abol
Bridge

Mount
Katahdin

Millinocket

Caratunk

Rangeley

Chairback Mtn

Monson

Saddleback Mtn

The Hiker Hut

Mount Washington

Rattle River
Hostel

Cascade Brook

Pinkham Notch

Killington
Peak

Hanover

Mount Moosilaukee

NEW YORK

NEW
HAMPSHIRE

Mount Greylock

Hudson R.

Cheshire

PENNSYLVANIA

MASSACHUSETTS

Harriman
SP

Bear Mtn

Stroudsburg

Sunfish
Pond

Kent

Delaware
Water Gap

CONNECTICUT

Edge of the
Woods
Outfitters

RHODE
ISLAND

NEW
JERSEY

DELAWARE

MARYLAND

Atlantic Ocean

○ Town

● Point of Interest

▲ Peak

Appalachian Trail

N

0   100   200 mi

0   100   200 km

"Follow the Appalachian Trail. . . . It cannot be followed on horse or
    awheel.
Remote for detachment, narrow for chosen company, winding for leisure,
lonely for contemplation, it beckons not merely north and south
but upward to the body, mind and soul of man."

—*Myron Avery*, In the Maine Woods

THE LIMIT

August 2013

I WENT TO THE Pacific Crest Trail to find my limit. I'd imagined my fastest known time attempt ending with me on hands and knees—dry heaving—at my utmost breaking point. Yet that never happened. I started the hike with my little plastic trowel, intent on digging deep as I'd learned to do over many ultramarathons, but the PCT laughed at that, and within a few days had handed me a full-size shovel instead.

Dig with this, it said.

Every day I hollowed myself out deeper and deeper. The sleep deprivation piled up, the calorie deficit compounded, and the wear and tear on my body increased. Every day was just a little harder than the day before. At the end of each—long after darkness fell—I stood panting, unable to fathom digging any more. I was empty, devoid of strength. But no matter the difficulty, I still had desire—to meet the goal, to reach the border, to cover the miles. And so, I journeyed farther into myself than ever before.

Many times I thought I saw my limit, a shadow in my periphery as I dug through layers of strength and willpower. Yet, I never found it. It was ephemeral, though I knew it must exist. I sought it in every climb, in every mile beyond forty I hiked in a day. I sought it in the pouring rain and hail, in the blistering triple-digit heat. I sought it when I was dizzy with thirst or hunger. I sought it even when my quads began to weaken in the last eight hundred miles, when my hamstring locked up and for a week I was unable to bend down to tie my shoe. But I simply could not find my limit, and after 1,900 miles I realized why.

My limit wasn't a wall. It wasn't a point of no return where I would lie on the ground in the fetal position unable to continue. My limit was an ephemeral shadow that recoiled, reformed, and retreated, leaving me to dig even deeper. I learned that it was a game of cat and mouse I'd agreed to without knowing the rules. At first I felt betrayed, but eventually I realized that this relentless search enabled me to move forward inexorably. Dumbfounded, I saw that my limit had not been a finite destination, but rather a daily achievement.

Now home in Washington State, only a few weeks away from the daily effort of the trail, I needed to recover from the quest to find my limit. But I also needed to prod at where it resided in the shadows, to reassure myself that what I'd found was real. I needed to redefine it.

I ran the dark path alongside Bellingham Bay with no head-lamp. Keenly aware of the stars above, the water to the west, and the moonrise in the east, my feet lifted and struck in rhythm, landing in blind faith on an Earth I trusted was there. Centering my gaze on the black horizon, and my thoughts on my breathing, I leaned into the run, ignoring the protests of my legs. I sought what I'd felt in those final miles of the Pacific Crest Trail. It hurt, but inside me a mantra blossomed: *I have an incomprehensible ability to suffer.*

I ran up Taylor Dock at full speed. My quads quivered with the need to give in. My lungs ached and a metallic taste rose in my mouth. I faltered. The taste brought up memories of gushing nosebleeds every day for a month as I hiked through the arid regions of the PCT, and how, unable to stop them, I'd tipped my head back, drinking my own blood until I wanted to vomit. Then leaning forward while I walked and watching fat, red droplets plummet to the sand in little puffs of dust, I choked on the memory.

I have an incomprehensible ability to suffer. Incomprehensible even to me. Run.

I reached the car, rubber legged and gasping. I'd discovered that the problem with proving you are capable of more than you believed possible is that you no longer have excuses, only reasons to push harder. *How can I possibly push harder than I already have?*

RESTLESSNESS 2

WATCHING THE PALE-GOLD HARVEST moon crest the foothills as I drove home, I recalled the last full moonrise I'd seen while crossing the flanks of North Sister in central Oregon. Its beams had turned Obsidian Falls into a ghostly veil as the water plummeted over the brink—the only sound in a silent wilderness. I remembered how I'd walked through fields of obsidian, like glittering black diamonds under my feet. Then I turned into my driveway, and blinked back the tears. My body was here, but my heart remained in the wild.

A few weeks after my run along Bellingham Bay, I found myself driving upriver at dusk, thinking existential thoughts as I gained on the mountains. Moments from the PCT replayed themselves on the movie screen inside my mind. I sang along as the radio proclaimed, "Nothing scares me anymore," the only phrase I could identify with in an ocean of vapid lyrics.

I found a comfortable spot to sleep a stone's throw from the trailhead, but the roar of Canyon Creek kept me awake. Five thirty arrived as it always did—too early—and I ate an almond butter sandwich in the pre-dawn light. It was the most normal thing I'd done since reaching Canada over a month before.

My dreadlocks, swollen by the humid air, bounced freely against the back of my neck as I ran along a ridge bathed in mid-day sun. The arduous climb up to McMillan Park had felt abnormally swift. Over and over I checked in with my body, awed at how effortless it felt to run through the mountains.

My body must be recovered from the PCT because it's handling this forty-mile run today as though it is nothing.

I didn't push. I simply reveled in the beauty of the wild and my body moving through it—free of the weight of a backpack. I was vaguely aware of reaching landmarks sooner than I expected, but it didn't really matter. I was home—wild and free—in a hazy realm of sunshine and weightlessness. Less than eleven hours later my feet pummeled the mighty bridge over boisterous Canyon Creek. I whooped with the joy of it and worked my way down to the rocky shoreline. Fully clad, I lay down in the glacial creek, letting the water roll over me until I went numb. My joy flowed downstream, draining from my heart and limbs along with the heat of my effort. Instead of sleeping at the trailhead again, I would drive downriver to a cabin beneath the cedars and fall asleep in a bed. Tomorrow, there would be no wandering in the alpine. Shivering, I headed for the car.

～

There is an ebb and a flow to life post-hike. I feel moments of utmost contentment, knowing that I accomplished something mind-boggling, whereas other moments I gaze out the window, wondering if I merely dreamt it. In still other moments, the absence of focus, miles, and freedom to walk sends me spiraling into despair, and I grieve. Life feels empty when the trail is over, even when it's full. The memories are like those of a loved one who is gone forever—with a churning in my stomach and an ache in my soul mixed with bittersweet joy. Having loved and lost—having hiked and come home—is better than never having hiked at all. Only time, and perhaps another journey, can mend the wound, though I know I'll be scarred forever. I say, "Never again," over and over, but it is a lie, a lie I tell myself when the grief overwhelms me. In the end, my memories of the trail are what make me feel whole. Despite the scars, loss, and depression, I know I will seek it again. For the joy, beauty, focus, drive, depletion, pain, and chance to achieve the impossible are simply too alluring. Just as I cannot hike forever, neither can I walk away for good.

Within the first week of finishing the PCT, I had stopped reading the comments of online articles about my fastest known time. The viciousness of internet personas both mystified and wounded me. Why critique the hike of someone they didn't even know? Or speculate about my motivations? My choices? Yet, I continued to answer the email requests to speak about my hike from Scouts, hiking clubs, schools, and outdoor stores. Each time I recounted my story the trail felt so real I could nearly hold it in my hand. But then I would go home and it slipped away, sand between my fingers. Lying awake in bed afterward, I would clench my fists, trying to sense it again.

I began to collect print articles about my hike in a shoebox under my bed, which quickly overflowed. The articles filled me with a sense of wonder. The woman they described sounded superhuman. Her story was incredible. And she was a complete stranger. One even stated that my life prior to setting the record was unremarkable. As though I had simply appeared out of nowhere to hike the entire PCT in 60 days, 17 hours, and 12 minutes.

Perhaps she *was* a superhuman stranger. Had I made her up? I was weak. I was always the mid-pack runner in every race. I labored to keep up on the ascents. My body was too broken. I'd been sick and out of shape when I'd started my hike. I could not be that woman.

Yet I could remember every detail with wrenching clarity. Each moment of every day was permanently etched into my memory. I could sit and write for hours, recalling every second. But perhaps the record had been an accident. Maybe the reason I didn't recognize that woman was because I knew that I wouldn't have succeeded without more than a fair amount of luck.

To find Anish—the woman I was on the trail—I knew that I had to once again reach my limit. Only then could I ask her whether the record had been an accident, whether she and I were truly the same person. Although I'd lost her to daily life, that woman from the magazine articles must exist inside me somewhere. And only she could quell my fears.

Everyone I met clamored to know what was next. As though I owed the world an encore, as though putting myself through the travails of transformation once was not enough. Maybe they were right. Maybe I did owe them—and myself—that encore. To prove I was no accident.

JOHN MUIR
TRAIL ATTEMPT

TEN MONTHS AFTER SETTING the self-supported fastest known time on the PCT, I decided to attempt the unsupported FKT on the John Muir Trail. Looking at my backpack as I sat in my Whitney Portal campsite at 8,374 feet, the burden to prove something weighed heavily on me. The backpack held nothing more than some food and a lot of desire, but it was everything I needed for the hike. Unlike a self-supported effort, where I could acquire supplies along the way, this time I would be entirely self-contained, start to finish. My body felt like it had recovered from the previous summer, but my mind was still clouded with doubts.

I would start up Mount Whitney in the wee hours, and from that summit attempt to run the 211 miles to Yosemite Valley in less than three and a half days to break the men's and women's FKTs. The setting sun turned the peaks around me pink. I gazed at them, knowing that I was here to fully immerse myself into the glorious, wild landscape ahead of me, much of it already familiar where the JMT ran congruent with the PCT. After I left camp in the morning, my plan was to not sleep until I'd seen it all, and drunk it all in. I desired to be alone with the mountains, but I was also terrified of failing and finding out that Anish, the FKT setter, was a fluke. I secured everything in the bear locker and crawled into my tent.

I slept fitfully. Fear had never kept me up before. I awoke at 2:26 a.m. and crawled out of my sleeping bag. Shoving a muffin down my throat, I turned on the SPOT, a personal locator beacon that would track my efforts, and in the warm darkness headed up toward the highest point in the Lower 48.

The climb started out feeling easy. I didn't have any trouble breathing or an excessive heart rate. My watch beeped, telling me to eat, and I was surprised that I had to force myself—I knew I should be hungry. I passed dozens of hiking parties on my way up the mountain. By the time I reached 13,000 feet in elevation my head felt fuzzy, as though I hadn't slept in a week. My heart pounded in my temples, and a small stabbing pain in the front of my head told me I needed more oxygen. By 14,000 feet my legs felt wobbly and I grew dizzy. In another 500 feet, I reached the benchmark on the summit. There, I plopped down and made myself eat something, even though I was so nauseous I could barely swallow without wanting to vomit. My legs were weak; the dizziness and fog in my brain was worse. I looked at my watch. It had taken me less than five hours to complete the eleven-mile approach. Now, the 211 miles to Yosemite Valley could begin. I stood up and headed down Mount Whitney—running.

I ran past the people I'd already passed on the way up that morning. Many cheered for me and gave me high fives even though they had no idea what I was actually doing. To them I was a woman in a dress running down a 14,000-foot moun-tain. I reached the intersection for the Whitney Portal Trail I'd ascended and turned right onto the John Muir Trail. Less than an hour later I was at Guitar Lake. Again, I tried to eat. I gagged and couldn't swallow. More oddly, I wasn't experiencing hun-ger pangs even though I'd been moving for approximately eight hours. I decided to stop forcing it, and trust my body to tell me when it needed food, as it had when my appetite faltered in the desert on the PCT.

Hours later, as I ascended to Bighorn Plateau, I stared up at a tiny notch in a formidable rock wall. The streak of snow clinging to the rock below the pass was a familiar face. Forester Pass looked impossible—as it always did—and yet I knew that it wasn't. To reach the switchbacks blasted from vertiginous rock walls, I passed through the tarns below the ice chute and then began to climb. Immediately I felt my pulse pound in my temples. I stopped and put my hands on my knees, head down. Holding still, I breathed deeply for thirty seconds before continuing.

Reaching the pass, I sat down on a rock to rest for the first time since the summit of Whitney. Though still not hungry, I was desperately thirsty, even though I'd been drinking. Combined with the heat and exertion, the arid air of the High Sierra was dehydrating me faster than I could drink. Downing what little water I had left, I plunged into the snow and made a beeline for the bare switchbacks far below. Back on clear trail, I again started to run.

The descent from Forester is long, even while running. Down, down, down I went, into a deep valley. It seemed that only recently I had been here, uncertain as to whether or not I was going to set the PCT record. Now I ran toward another record, to convince myself that I deserved the last one. My head swam with altitude and irony. I reached the junction and turned to climb toward Glen Pass, but I simply couldn't. Sitting down, I tried to eat, but couldn't do that either. No matter what I tried to put in my body, it came back out. I'd been on the move for sixteen hours.

I climbed slowly, stopping frequently to catch my breath while I gazed down at Charlotte Lake. A year ago, I'd been awestruck by its sparkling beauty. This time—though I was there at the same time of day with the same golden Sierra light pouring over everything—the lake looked dull and lifeless. I climbed on.

Sunset grew nigh as I pushed upward into the rocky basin south of Glen Pass. I ground to a shuffle as I climbed, unable to breathe. My heart was pounding so hard, I expected to go into arrhythmia. I stopped often. My legs were weak. My head spun. The top looked so far away. Yet, I knew there was snow on the north slope. I had to get over the pass before nightfall so I wouldn't be route-finding on icy snow in the dark. Out of water and still unable to eat, I pushed forward, counting breaths and footsteps to take my focus off my body.

I reached the top as the horizon sucked the last rays of light out of the sky. There was indeed snow—more than I had anticipated. Squinting, I tried to recall the course of the descent. A large step took me across the moat separating the rocks at the top of the pass from the boot pack entrenched in the snow on the downward slope. I slipped many times as I followed the tracks leading from bare rock to bare rock. At each, I looked for a cairn—when there was none, I would guess and pick my way across snow once more. Slowly I wound down from the pass. Water poured from under a rock and I drank with gulps of desperation. Finally, I crossed the ribbon of indigo water that connected the Rae Lakes before plowing into the winding terrain on the other side.

"There is a spring coming up," I told myself out loud. "It's just ahead. Not much farther."

I reached it and filled my bottle and water bladder. I drank—then I drank more. My kidneys ached, but I reassured myself that it was from my pack bouncing against my back. It was a lie to keep my mind from panicking about muscle death induced rhabdomyolysis or subsequent renal failure. There were always mental games to play when I knew I was going onward regardless.

I tried to run. *I should be able to run!* The miles descending alongside Woods Creek were easy. Instead I hiked, reaching the camp near the suspension bridge across it at midnight. I simply couldn't fathom going any farther without sleep. The ascent up the Whitney Portal Trail seemed ages ago. I sat down and napped for ten minutes, then got up and began the climb to Pinchot Pass.

I'd run through the dead of night many times before, yet this time was much more difficult. I stopped frequently to catch my breath, and my progress grew tremendously slow. I crossed the twenty-four-hour mark still unable to eat. My mind wandered to other things. It was a blessed feeling to think of something beyond my present suffering, but I fought it. *I cannot stop focusing. I'm barely a third of the way.*

The sliver moon rose and I clicked off my headlamp. I stood in the absolute blackness and gazed up at the Milky Way slicing the star-riddled sky. Aware that I was staring at the edge of the galaxy in more ways than one, I took a deep breath, cementing that moment in my mind forever. Then I moved on.

As the light turned gray, the hallucinations began. Every tree was a person. Every rock, a tent. I started seeing people where there was nothing to shape-shift. I couldn't tell what was real and what wasn't. But it didn't matter. I believed in the trail under my feet, my breathing, the movement, the nausea, the waves of exhaustion . . . all of that was real. The miles and miles ahead of me, the passes left to climb, the thousands of feet of elevation gain—those were real.

At the top of Pinchot Pass I turned on my music for the first time. I started running, increasing the volume to drown out the pounding of my heart—and to keep me conscious. I ran and ran and ran. The hallucinations faded somewhat. After I crossed the South Fork of the King River I turned the music off and resumed climbing.

I passed thru-hikers breaking camp and soon they were behind me in a line as we crossed tree line and strode across rocky plains. Then the hallucinations returned, fast and furious, as fatigue made me dizzy. Finally, without preamble, I stepped aside and sat down. The thru-hikers passed me and I closed my eyes. Five minutes later I snapped awake, reminded that I had to press onward. I rose to my feet.

As I walked, the shadows and rocks jutting out from the wall ahead of me suddenly shifted into the biggest cottonwood tree imaginable, seemingly 2,000 feet high. I blinked and shook my head, but it remained. It looked like those dot paintings from the early '90s with 3D images that pop out when you stare long enough. I looked down at my dusty trail running shoes rhythmically striking the ground. When I looked back up, the tree was the side of a mountain again. I squinted. Now, a tree. I continued to play with my vision, watching the hallucination appear and then vanish, as I walked across the barren landscape. The trail turned and began to ascend. Looking upward, I was discouraged by the thousands of vertical feet spiraling above me.

I reached the end of the switchback, bent over at the waist, placed my hands on my knees and lowered my head. Breathing deeply into my belly, I waited for the spinning behind my eyes to subside. I counted breaths. After forty-five I could no longer feel my heart trying to escape my chest. I straightened, and waited a moment to let the blood pressure equalize. The end of the switchback was fifty yards ahead. "I only have to walk to there," I said.

I repeated this technique over and over and over and over as I ascended from the valley floor to the rocky heights of Mather Pass. Three switchbacks from the top, I mustered my strength and walked again, head down, staring at my feet. A few yards from the turn of the switchback, I glanced up from my feet to see a cinnamon bear with chocolate paws and ears clambering toward me, cutting up from the switchback below. I stared at the hallucination as it turned toward me, a mere ten feet away. I could see the texture of the fur, the annoyance in its eyes . . .

"Hughhhh!" the bear huffed as it started toward me, eyes locked on mine.

I blinked, my mind moving slowly. *I would hallucinate a happy bear, not an angry bear. This is not a hallucination!*

I backed away. The bear followed me, and not slowly. I did not trust myself to walk backward without tripping so I turned sideways and shuffled away, looking in its direction but no longer allowing it to make eye contact. I reached the end of the switchback and scooped up two medium-sized rocks as I clambered off the end of the trail, then turned to face the approaching bear.

"BEAR!!!!!!!" a woman yelled from above me, confirming it wasn't a hallucination.

The bear stopped walking toward me and looked up. It tried to climb up between the switchbacks, but slid back. Walking a few more steps toward me, the bear tried again to cut the switchback. This time it was successful. With a burst of incredible power, it bolted along the trail, off the end of the switchback above me, and across the rocks—disappearing over the pass.

I looked at the trail I'd walked already and then ceded to the bear. *I have to repeat the switchback.* I sighed and dropped the rocks.

A few minutes later, I sat on Mather Pass and closed my eyes. My head swam. *I need sleep. I've got altitude sickness.* I looked down at my hands—they were purple. My body had prioritized circulating oxygen to my working muscles at the expense of my extremities many hours ago. My kidneys ached. I tried to remember the last time I'd peed and couldn't. In fact, I couldn't remember much of anything. I tried to talk to the group of thru-hikers who'd arrived minutes after me, but forgot what I'd said as soon as I'd spoken. A few moments later I started my descent toward the Golden Staircase. *I can't stop. Not if I want to break this record. And I need to know my answer. I can't stop until I know.*

When the trail flattened out, I ran. I reached the tightly packed switchbacks of the Golden Staircase and turned on my music. As I traversed the flatland that led to Le Conte Canyon, I wondered who the woman running alongside me was and why she couldn't run any faster. If it weren't for her I was certain I could have run so much faster. Why I was running with her wasn't clear, but somehow, I knew I had to stay with her—no matter how slow she was moving. After a few miles a realization came crashing through the fog in my mind: *I AM that woman.*

The clarity was immediately followed by two confusing questions. *Who am I? Where am I?*

I ran in a daze as I pondered, but I simply did not know. Floating alongside myself, watching my body struggle, I was happy to be weightless and unable to feel its pain. Finally, I remembered the answers to my two questions, pulled from some far depth of memory that seemed incredibly difficult to access. *I am Heather Anderson. I am running the JMT in California.*

My mind was a frayed wire, barely connected to my body. From the safety of examining my situation beyond the confines of a corporeal husk, I could understand that my disassociation indicated I might be in serious trouble. I'd never come close to having an out-of-body experience before, not even while running the hardest ultra-marathons or during the PCT FKT. *Is this what it's like to die?* I thought about snipping that frayed wire and drifting away, up and over the Sierra. To be free in the mountains in a way I'd never been before.

I came back to myself abruptly, and found that I was wading deeply through the symptoms of altitude sickness. Their severity was surprising—brought into stark relief by the reprieve I'd just experienced. My kidneys were stressed. My lungs and chest ached. A rattly, wet cough had begun. I knew my body was circulating oxygen to my moving muscles at the expense of everything else, including my digestive tract and extremities— maybe even my brain. A lack of calories was also taking its toll, and I could not go any longer without sleeping. Spotting a level area beneath a pine tree three yards off the trail, I climbed up to it. There, I lay down and closed my eyes, giving myself permission to sleep for two hours. Consciousness left me almost immediately.

I snapped awake an hour later. After putting on my shoes and getting to my feet, I looked down, surprised and relieved to see that my hands were pink and healthy looking. I felt alert as I hiked. *All I needed was sleep. I'm fine now.* A few minutes later, I met two thru-hikers—Willie and Carson. We fell in stride together, chatting as we climbed toward Muir Pass. Moving three miles per hour for the first time since the earliest miles of the JMT, I felt normal. When we stopped for water, they paused to filter, while I simply dipped my bottles in and continued on. I did not care about the long-term risk of Giardia; I just needed to survive the next one hundred miles.

An hour or so later the rejuvenation ran out and my pace slowed. I was well into the rocky, lake-riddled terrain dominating the southern approach to Muir Pass. My chest ached like it had never ached before. My hands were a dusky purple again. I went into yet another coughing fit. Phlegm shot out of my mouth and I stared at where it lay, blood red like a ruby, on the ground. I looked up at the ridges far above me before taking a deep breath, and walking on.

A few minutes later Carson caught up to me.

"Where's Willie?" I said.

"He stopped to eat. I figured if Anish can do this without eating so can I. Mind if I hike with you?"

"Not at all. I'm just going really slowly now. I ran out of energy. And I just coughed up something red. It looked like blood."

He was silent for a little while. "I don't mind this pace."

We walked on, talking about the mundane topics thru-hikers talk about.

"What do you do for a living?" I asked.

"I'm a paramedic."

I laughed, which turned into that same wheezing cough. "So, you know all about coughing up blood, don't you?"

"Yeah. Do you have any burning in your chest?"

"Not burning, per se. My lungs are just sore. Like an over-worked muscle. I think maybe it was just from all the dry air and dust."

He was quiet for a minute. "Yeah, maybe. I'd say if it happens again you should go to the hospital."

We began to lose the trail in the rocks and runoff, wandering and problem solving together. Every once in a while, I would say, "Oh! I made this mistake last year. The trail is over there."

Darkness fell before we reached Helen Lake, and I knew I was moving at a glacial pace. Willie caught up.

"I have to sit down," I said. "You guys go on ahead."

"Nope, we'll wait."

Twice more I stopped to sit and tried to send them on. Carson assured me, "I *want* to wait." I stopped apologizing and instead was thankful for the company.

We reached the top of Muir Pass just before eleven. When we stepped into the hut, I was surprised at how warm the half dozen sleeping hikers inside had made it. Willie and Carson went about setting out their bags and preparing for bed. I took a bite of a bar and sat down next to the door, leaning against my pack. I closed my eyes and slept.

Thirty minutes later I woke up, and took another bite of the bar. One bite at a time was all I could manage. It had been taking me seven to ten hours to finish a bar over the last twenty-four hours, rather than eating the allocated bar-per-hour. I fell asleep for another fifteen minutes. The next time I woke up, I stood, swung the door open quietly, and stepped out into the brisk midnight air. I knew I had crossed a threshold—now my very life was in danger. Yet I couldn't relent, not now. Leaving Muir Hut, I was driven not only to find an answer, but to follow the trail as it dropped thousands of feet. *The only cure for altitude sickness is to go down.*

I staggered down the pass, crisscrossing between tarns and rocky flats. After crossing Evolution Creek—tired of stumbling and tripping—I sat down and fell asleep for five minutes. Walking again, I felt demoralized. There was so much more climbing on the twenty-mile descent than I remembered. I'd been counting on moving faster through here and getting to a lower elevation quickly. When I tripped and nearly fell into large, silent Wanda Lake just inches off trail, I realized I'd fallen asleep while walking. Scared, I sat down and napped again.

Ten minutes later, I awoke and realized I couldn't remember which direction I'd come from. I consulted the Halfmile navigation app, and was thankful I'd double-checked, since I'd started out facing the wrong way. Soon I was walking alongside a beautiful, but stygian, lake. The stars twinkled on the water's surface in a mesmerizing fashion. Suddenly I realized it was the lake I'd almost fallen into.

I stopped, confused, and looked down . . . there were my footprints going the opposite way. I looked at Halfmile and obligingly backtracked. I looked at Halfmile again, confused. I started to cry. "I KNOW I passed this lake going the other way!"

No matter how my fuzzy mind contorted, there was no way I could understand what was going on. *Halfmile must be wrong. There must be a glitch.* I pulled out my compass. The needle spun and pointed in the same direction Halfmile said to go.

"No, no, no . . ." I said adamantly.

I knew—no matter what my frazzled brain believed—I had to trust my instruments. I knew the compass and the Halfmile app weren't wrong. I walked back past Wanda Lake for the third time that night as the first blush of light tinged the horizon to my right. I realized vaguely that after my first five-minute nap I must've turned the wrong way and walked for over an hour back toward the pass, hence the unexpected amount of uphill effort.

Light came and I tried to run. I kept waking up to find myself standing in bushes off the trail, not knowing how I got there. Then I would realize I'd traveled one hundred yards from where I last remembered being awake. Over and over I slept while moving; once I even started drooling as though I'd been asleep with my mouth open, face-first into a pillow.

I knew I needed rest, but I wouldn't be able to sleep for long—I was too cold. And even a dozen five-minute catnaps wouldn't be enough. I reached the major ford of Evolution Creek, climbed onto a high bank, and looked into the water. I picked a line that avoided the deepest holes and plunged in. The frigid water numbed my feet and awakened my mind. I sloshed out on the opposite side, thankful that every time I'd crossed this creek over the years, I'd avoided getting washed downstream toward the fatal falls.

I ran and hiked onward. As the day grew warmer and my elevation dropped, I grew stronger. When at last it was warm enough for me to sleep, I found a flat spot and lay down. I wanted a two-hour nap before climbing Selden Pass, but slept for only fifteen minutes. When I was unable to fall back asleep, I continued on. While the lower elevation meant I wasn't coughing as much, the cumulative exertion and sleeplessness were still taking their toll. I took a bite of a bar every hour and began to drink more, not bothering to filter. My kidneys stopped aching and I rejoiced in the simple fact that I needed to urinate for the first time in nearly two days. At the pass, I dropped to the ground and slept for five minutes. Then I got up and descended to Bear Creek.

My mind had often left my body over the last thirty-six hours. I wasn't even sure how long it had been since I began my attempt at the fastest known time. I tried to count the days and miles remaining. *About one hundred miles. Maybe two and a half days?*

I realized I was on pace to break the women's unsupported record by a day and a half. I wouldn't be bringing the parity that I'd hoped for to the three-day gap between the men's and women's records, but it was something. I felt slightly better. Two bites of bar an hour. No gasping for air. Nine thousand feet felt so good.

I can still do this. The danger is past now, right? I fleetingly thought of how I'd run off the trail repeatedly in the early morning darkness. How I'd nearly fallen into a lake. The moment I almost lost my balance and plunged off a cliff somewhere in the night. The fatigue would only get worse. My calorie deficit was already immense. *But I can do this. I can suffer more. I can suffer longer.*

In my mind, I composed the text I'd send from the dead-end road outpost of Reds Meadow—the only place with cell reception on the entire trail—recounting the trauma I'd been through, but sharing that I was continuing on. That way my boyfriend would know why it was taking me so damn long. *I know I can suffer more. I know I can suffer longer. But do I want to?*

A jarring sound brought my wandering thoughts back to the moment. I stared down at my pocket. The noise came again. *A text?* I pulled out my phone, which should have been off. I sat down on a log and opened the good luck texts from my boyfriend. I blurted out what had been happening in one verbose, rambling text. Followed by the words, "I can still do this though," added more to convince myself than him.

The worry I read in the text I received back cut through the stubbornness and the fog in my brain. He threatened to call search and rescue if I did not quit. Finally acquiescing to the severity of my situation, I responded with what I knew was the proper choice, "I need to quit. But I am going to self-extract at Reds Meadow."

After fording Bear Creek, I climbed up and over Bear Ridge and descended steeply into the deep drainage of Mono Creek. I still floated, barely connected to my struggling body. At half past nine I found a sprawling tree and crawled under it, wrapped up in my emergency blanket and all my clothes. I knew I wasn't generating enough body heat because I was depleted, but there was no way I could climb Silver Pass without some sleep. I set my alarm for two hours later and hoped I wasn't going to pop awake after a few minutes.

When the alarm rang, I clenched my eyes tightly closed. Then I sat up and realized I was lying beneath a tree, my cell phone chiming merrily. Cognizance of what I was doing came back and I shut the alarm off. Something about deciding to quit had given me the permission to fully rest. *Only thirty-five miles to Reds Meadow.* I switched the SPOT to tracking so that if I didn't arrive my ground crew could find me, and got up.

Shivering, I decided to leave my down jacket, balaclava, hat, mittens, wool pants, and dress on until the climb warmed me. When it didn't, I wrapped the emergency blanket around me like a . . . I strained to think of the word. It took me fifteen minutes to come up with it: sarong.

I staggered through the dark, cursing the many false summits of Silver Pass. At every bend I hoped I was at the top. I thought it was a 10,000-foot pass, but I passed the 10,000-foot sign and the trail showed no signs of topping out. My cough came back. I spit out phlegm, but none of it was red. I needed to get out. At last I crested the pass. I didn't even slow down.

Eventually the sun came up and I took off the emergency blanket. I allowed my mind to wander, to do whatever it needed to do to keep me conscious and moving. I wouldn't sleep again. I was quitting. I just needed to reach Reds Meadow. *Only twenty-five more miles.*

Midday I reached the Reds Meadow complex and bought a bottle of water from the tiny store. The shuttle bus to Mammoth pulled in moments later and I boarded, sitting down and guzzling cold water as we pulled away from the cluster of cabins. Rolling down the mountain road, I didn't look back. I felt no regret—only blunt acceptance of my failure.

R E C L A M A T I O N

ONLY IN THE WEEKS that followed—after my body had healed—
did I realize how deeply I'd failed. I'd been willing to literally run
myself to death, and yet I hadn't even come close to setting a new
record. I'd also failed by believing that I needed to prove something to other people. If I could accept that my PCT record was
a one-time thing, a fluke, then what should it matter whether
other people believed in me? Proving them wrong wasn't worth
risking my health.

I spent my birthday alone in a hotel room in Colorado where
I was attending a conference. I stared at myself in the mirror, at
the dreadlocks crowning my head. They had begun a smidgen
more than a year ago, when I was struggling through the desert on the PCT, then whipped into tighter locks in the winds of
the High Sierra. I'd separated the dreads with vicious tugs as I
walked across the monotonous miles of Oregon, but they'd grown
thicker as I'd grown stronger. As the invisible miles behind me
piled up, my dreads were a physical reminder of the passage of
time and the distance I had covered. Their creation was bound
with my own rebirth.

Because of them, I'd seen the PCT every time I looked into the mirror over the last year. Every day I'd carried that trail experience with me in a visible, defining way. Yet the face looking back was still a stranger. I couldn't do it again. I couldn't set a second record. The PCT had been a fluke. It had been an accident.

"You're a charlatan, Anish. You were just *lucky*," I told my reflection.

I buried my face in my hands and sobbed. I was not capable of breaking a record. I was still nothing. Perhaps, as I'd learned the previous summer, I did belong in the mountains and it was ok that I was only happy there. I could accept myself for what I was, but I also needed to accept what I was not: I was not an athlete. I was not a success. I was not special. I never would be.

The tears eventually tapered off. The PCT was all I'd lived and breathed for two months in 2013, but it had haunted me every day since I drove away from Manning Park, at the end of the trail. I was called The Ghost by people who followed my hike online, but the real specter was the trail itself. I began to hack the dreads out of my hair with a small pair of scissors, a nail file, and my fingers. They figuratively held the sweat, dirt, blood, tears, and emotion of thousands of miles of the PCT. They had to go.

"I can no longer let this one thing define me." I spoke aloud to reinforce my resolve as I pulled another severed dreadlock out of my hair and threw it into the trash can. "No matter what any magazine author may say, my other hikes, my races, my life before the summer of 2013 *was* notable. It mattered. Maybe not to the world, but to me. Achieving the Triple Crown by the age of twenty-five was significant. The fact that my first successful multinight backpacking trip was the AT is notable. The fact that I did it in four months, despite being overweight and out of shape the year before, was amazing. Placing fourth in my first one-hundred-mile race was notable. Completing five one-hundred-mile races in one year when I was so injured that

I hardly ran between them is incredible. Those things matter to *me*."

Many times I'd felt my life ended when I reached the PCT's northern terminus at the border with Canada, that my purpose on Earth was complete. My post-hike depression had swallowed me whole when I fought to find meaning beyond my PCT FKT. Now I was certain I could not let it become the only important thing I achieved.

After my spectacular failure on the JMT, I was finally realizing that forcing myself into the spotlight again and again had not helped me cope—and neither had seeing the locks, formed through toil and perseverance, every time I looked in the mirror. The PCT record was not the only thing that mattered about Heather Anderson. It took failing at the JMT record to find the temerity to stand in a hotel room and cut away the visible remnants of the FKT.

"I am not invincible. I am not perfect. I am human. I have dreams beyond what anyone else cares about. Aspirations no one will report in a magazine or mention on their Twitter feeds."

Two and a half hours later, I ran a disposable hotel comb through what was left of my hair for the first time in fourteen months.

"I am moving on. I have reached the terminus again, only this time I am walking away without looking back."

I vowed that I would never again speak publicly about my 2013 PCT hike. I would trade distance hiking and running for mountaineering. And I would heal. The comb snagged on the one small dread I'd left in the back, underneath the rest of my hair. I couldn't see it, but I would always know it was there—just like what I'd done the previous summer.

HOMESICK 5

SIX MONTHS PASSED IN a metronomic rhythm. I went about the routine of life: coffee, breakfast, and work, with my spare time spent either climbing peaks or planning my next climb. Yet night after night I woke with adrenaline coursing through my body. I sat bolt upright in bed breathing hard and trying to bring myself back into the reality of a bedroom where I was safe—to calm my brain as it tried to synthesize the nightmarish dream world I'd just been in with where my body was.

The details of the dreams varied, but the theme was always the same: failed attempts at backpacking. In some dreams I was poisoned. In others I was attacked by animals, or shot. Always, the calamity befell me as I tried to run to the mountains. Then I would wake up and sit in the darkness, hugging my knees as tears rolled down my cheeks. I desperately desired the life of the trail. I needed to walk day after day through the wilderness.

On December 31, 2014, I dreamed the most powerful dream of all. I'd loaded my backpack and started out the door, but then I remembered I had to go to work. Three employers were yelling at me because I was late. Within the dream, I woke up to the sun streaming in my face and birds chirping outside. Lying there, I imagined I was in my tent. I stealthily grabbed my pack and snuck out the door—away from employers and nightmares. I climbed into a yellow cab and was soon trotting across red clay earth in search of white blazes. At a junction in a clearing I found them. With a wide smile, I flung my arms open and twirled in a circle. Then I merged onto the white-blazed path and didn't look back.

I woke from that dream within a dream—half nightmare, half vision—on January 1. There were no more dreams of a return to the trail after that. I now knew the path I must follow—one marked with white blazes.

PREPARATION 6

I'D CONTEMPLATED ATTEMPTING the self-supported speed record on the PCT for years. The thought of someday trying it had given me hope when my marriage dissolved, when other relationships ended, when I quit my job and wandered aimlessly for eight months. Always, the trail was there, as something I wanted to do, something I was terrified of, and yet something I was convinced I had to try. Always. Stepping away from the southern terminus at the start of the PCT had been the most terrifying moment of my life. Reaching the northern terminus—essentially rebirthed—had been the most visceral. Now, despite forswearing FKTs and, to some extent, long-distance hiking, the white blazes of the Appalachian Trail were inexplicably calling me.

"I can't believe I'm planning another two-thousand-plus-mile FKT," I muttered to myself as I ordered Awol's Appalachian Trail guidebook and downloaded the Guthook navigation app to my phone. A long row of Priority Mail Flat Rate boxes containing food, shoes, socks, and other supplies sat in the hallway, waiting to be taped shut and mailed. I sighed, turned off the light, and crawled into bed.

In the morning my boyfriend and I got in the car and headed north to Canada for a weeklong mountaineering trip. During that expedition, I couldn't shake the nagging feeling that I needed to call my mom. We returned to cell reception five days later, and the news that my mother had suffered a severe stroke the day we'd left for Canada.

~

Two weeks afterward, I stood in my parents' tiny living room, trying to explain my upcoming hike to my father.

"This is what I do now, Dad. I'm a professional hiker. I have sponsors helping me. If I set the AT record it will be a really big deal. I've put everything I have left into this hike." *I need this hike as much as I need food or air,* I added mentally.

"Are they paying you?"

"Well, no. I don't get paid. But they've donated gear and food to help me." I paused, searching for further words of explanation, and finding that I did not have them. "I just have to do this."

My father shrugged and leaned over the arm of his recliner to aim the remote at the TV behind me. The volume of *The Andy Griffith Show* rerun increased. Our conversation was clearly over. He'd spent thirty years building cars for General Motors, trading his time for a paycheck to sustain himself and his family. It was a tidy equation—one that was easy to understand. Yet, somehow, he'd raised a daughter who did not follow a neat mathematical path. Her rocky route was unfathomable to him.

I went into the dining room and sat at the table. Opening my laptop, I thought of my mother—in the hospital—barely able to speak. I thought about the rocks, roots, and mud that awaited me on the Appalachian Trail. Then I turned my mind to the process of planning my upcoming hike.

After numbing hours of scouring maps, plotting campsites, and making copious notes in my spreadsheets, I exhaled deeply and slipped into running shorts. Outside, in the oppressive humidity of the Midwestern summer, I ran down a dirt road, under a blue sky dotted with promising clouds.

As I ran, I passed corn fields bordered by ditches full of mullein, chicory, staghorn sumac, and Queen Anne's lace. It was a landscape familiar to me in ways the peaks of Washington were now. I felt a sense of home, just as I did on mountain trails. My feet rhythmically struck the packed dirt and I sweated profusely in the ninety-degree heat.

How can I feel at home in so many places? Even ones so different from each other? The stress flowed out of me and into the wide-open air as I ran. I knew that if my feet took me there, I could always find a home in nature.

A week later we brought my mother home from the hospital. I sat down across from her at the table and held her hand. It had been over a month since her stroke and she still struggled to find words and create sentences. I wondered if I'd ever be able to sit and talk freely with her again.

"Mom, it's time to go. I'm sorry I can't be here right now, but Dad and Sis will take care of you. You're going to be ok."

She nodded and squeezed my hand. "I know."

I'd offered to stay, but she'd insisted I go. As much as my father did not understand or support my path, my mother in more than equal measure did. She knew hiking was my life, even if she was worried—even though my dad could not comprehend it. She had known from the moment I took her to the white-blazed streets of Hot Springs, North Carolina in the fall of 2003 that I was meant to do something different: to walk a wild and mountainous path.

"I promise. This is the last time I try a multi-thousand-mile FKT. I promise."

I wrapped my arms around her and we cried. No matter how many times we bid goodbye to one another we always cried. The drumbeat of both our hearts had always been in sync. I vowed to never again ignore my gut if it told me to call home.

I turned to my dad and hugged him awkwardly. "Goodbye, Dad."

I picked up my backpack, and walked out the door.

~

The plane landed in Manchester, New Hampshire, a few hours later. My best friend, Apple Pie, and her husband, Greenleaf—both avid thru-hikers—picked me up at the curb and we headed north. The sun was shining and I marveled at the lushness of it all: the Oz-green landscape, thick deciduous timberlands, and the shining lakes and rivers. I felt a twinge of nostalgia. Here in the Appalachians, I was also home.

We made ourselves comfortable in a suite at a hostel in Millinocket, Maine. I laid out my gear: a Gossamer Gear 40-liter backpack, a Zpacks Solplex tent, a quart baggie of first aid supplies and ditties, two headlamps, a sleeping pad and bag, fleece sleep clothes, a rain jacket, poncho, trekking poles, a Sawyer Squeeze filter, and a few other things. One item at a time, I carefully repacked, trying to relax, but my body and mind were in overdrive. They knew what was coming. *I* knew what was coming. My resolve wavered, and I batted the ideas of quitting versus following through back and forth.

"What the hell am I doing?" I muttered to my gear.

I showered and lay down on the bed. I had no more confidence I could complete this FKT than when I left Campo to start the PCT two and a half years before. But I did have the same sense of destiny. I knew that I had to try. I would attempt to hike the 2,189-mile-long Appalachian Trail faster than anyone else had. I would do it alone and not to prove anything to anyone this time except myself—unlike the JMT, this hike was more than an attempted encore. It was eight months to the day from my dream of following the white blazes. There was something I needed to learn out there on the rocky, rooty trail.

"I just don't know what it is," I whispered, before closing my eyes and trying to sleep.

TRIAL BY WATER

ON SEPTEMBER 11, 2003, I stood at the base of Mount Katahdin in Maine, and signed the climbers register. It felt surreal to stand there, over 2,170 miles from where I'd started on Springer Mountain in Georgia exactly four months before. I was wiser to the world—and to the woods. I'd set out with no knowledge of backpacking and having spent most of my short life as an inactive couch potato. During the journey, my body had changed. No longer was I a soft, overweight flatlander. I was trail hardened—thirty pounds lighter and leaner. It hadn't come without a price, however. With a mere five hundred dollars to my name on Springer Mountain, I'd reached Katahdin without enough left to buy a bus ticket home. I was also malnourished from living on peanut butter, Pop-Tarts, candy, and the cast-offs found in hiker boxes and trash cans. I'd slogged through rivers and mud, and slept in the mouse-infested three-sided shelters sprinkled along the trail corridor as it wound through the ancient Appalachian Mountain range.

In a short time, I was atop the mountain and realized I hadn't met Destiny. Instead, I'd found Life. I was in love with the mountains—with living in nature. The cool, foggy air swirled lazily around the rocky peak as I walked to the six-foot-high summit cairn and reverently placed on it the stone I'd carried there from Georgia. I descended a new woman: a woman who called herself not Heather, but Anish.

~

I clambered past the dozens of people strewn about the Hunt Spur ridge on a sunny August Saturday. Grabbing the protruding rebar handles, I hauled myself up giant boulders—the knobby vertebrae of the sacred "Greatest Mountain." I hopped around hikers resting along the arduous ascent and bounded up the rocks, following white blazes. My heart pounded with adrenaline and the strain of a 5,000-foot climb to Baxter Peak, the summit of Maine's highest mountain—Mount Katahdin. Less than two hours after I'd left Apple Pie and Greenleaf's car, I was standing near a battered wooden sign. I was back. This time not as a northbounder, as most AT hikers were, but as a southbounder. I climbed the mountain not to end my hike, but to reach the start of it. It seemed fitting to begin where I'd stopped last time and tread backward—getting the hardest part of the trail out of the way first.

"Katahdin," I breathed the word softly.

I stood in the blowing fog and felt the two ends of my life meeting one another, creating a circle with a nearly audible click. I'd been barely twenty-two the last time I'd stood here, twelve years prior. After descending this mountain, I'd returned to Michigan—with the flavor of the Appalachians on my tongue and golden dreams of the mountain West in my mind. In the years after that first thru-hike, I'd never once thought I would stand at the top of Katahdin again. Yet, here I was.

The summit was quiet this morning. No noisy celebrations as there had been in September of 2003. Two northbound finishers sat by themselves near the summit sign. Behind a windbreak a few early hikers were enjoying a picnic—they'd obviously camped within the park and, unlike me, hadn't needed to wait in line for the entrance to open. Everyone else from the conga line of cars was now strung along the spine of rocks below—their colors and movements evocative of Tibetan prayer flags waving in the wind. I inhaled, mindful only of the mountain, the fog, and my thoughts.

For over a year after my first completion of the Appalachian Trail, I'd dwelled on one singular moment from that hike—one that took place as I'd sat facing the late afternoon sun on the Webster Cliffs in the White Mountains of New Hampshire. Fellow thru-hikers had told me there was another trail out there—in the mysterious West. A trail that wound a serpentine path from Mexico to Canada. A true wilderness without the excessive people of the Appalachians. A trail that forged its way through barren desert, crossed 12,000-foot-high passes bathed in snow, and followed a crest of unthinkable beauty through the lush, volcanic Pacific Northwest. It was the younger sister— gorgeous and untamed—of the Appalachian Trail. In the face of a red sunset on a late summer's day in New Hampshire, I'd known in my soul that I must hike the Pacific Crest Trail.

Now I'd hiked the PCT twice, each time seeking something radically different. My journeys on that once mysterious and beckoning trail had led me back here—to the older, wiser Appalachians and to the summit of Mount Katahdin. The wet, forested trail before me now was so unlike the dry, expansive Pacific Crest it was laughable. So possibly was my intent: to hike the AT faster than any other self-supported thru-hiker ever had. Just as on the PCT, I would have no crew, no support. When I made my way down the trail, I would be on my own: reliant on the boxes I had shipped to myself and purchases I would make along the way, able to accept only spontaneous kindness from strangers—trail magic. This time, though, I hoped to melt into the sheer numbers of AT hikers and not draw attention to my personal pilgrimage.

I knew I was not the woman who stepped off Mount Katahdin twelve years ago, but I was also not the same woman who walked the length of the Sierra and the Cascade Ranges in 2005 and 2013. I was a different person than when I followed the Continental Divide from Canada to Mexico in 2006, or when I was afraid to run my first 50K and my first hundred-mile race. The question of who I was now—after having reached Manning Park almost two years ago—remained unanswered. *I hope the answer is somewhere between here and Springer Mountain.*

Looking southward through clouds that parted intermittently, I glimpsed the lake-dotted Penobscot basin. In a few days I would cross it, passing by ponds separated by green humps blanketed with thick timber. I felt in over my head. Time and again my response when people had asked the inevitable "why?" about my PCT hike had been simply: "If you never risk biting off more than you can chew, then you'll never know how much you can handle." So here I was again, biting off more than I could probably chew. Matt Kirk's self-supported AT record was fifty-eight days. The supported record had been set just a few weeks before by Scott Jurek at forty-six days and change, breaking the previous record held by Jennifer Pharr Davis by a mere three hours.

"Do I really have any business trying this?" I wondered aloud. *I'm trying for closer to Scott and Jen's times than Matt's. It's insane.*

I was scared, not because of what I didn't know, but because of what I did. Stepping away from Campo in June of 2013 had been a terrifying leap into the unknown. Today, I would be stepping into the known as soon as I left the mountaintop. I knew I would be racing the clock. I knew I'd be forsaking sleep and pushing myself to the brink of starvation by burning more calories than I could ever possibly carry. I knew I was committing to relentless forward progress for 2,189 miles. It was a self-induced fight or flight.

I've failed at everything since I reached Canada. I'd been unable to complete the two most challenging things I'd attempted in the last two years: the Barkley, a notorious ultramarathon with more than fifty thousand feet of elevation gain, and the JMT FKT.

I spoke aloud again to reinforce my resolve. "If you're not scared, you aren't pushing yourself. If you're not pushing yourself, you're not going to expand your limits. You'd just be living in the realm of the safe and stagnate."

And nobody wants to be stagnant, I added mentally, pulling a chocolate bar out of my armpit where I'd been warming it since I'd reached the top. I was starting to shiver slightly in the cold clamminess. I wasn't really hungry, but I knew I had to force in calories—five hundred calories of chocolate in this case.

I reminded myself of the intention I'd written on the back of my resupply-box schedule: "I want to always be trying to grow and change and expand. I want to seek to be stronger, braver, and more courageous in everything from communicating to hiking. I can't let the past define me, but to do so, I need to create a new present and future."

I was not any of the women I'd been before. I was the sum of all those experiences. *But am I greater than the sum of the parts?* I needed to answer that question and others before I could move forward. My path had formed a circle and brought me back to the top of Mount Katahdin. It had led me to seek the hardships of an FKT a second time, because I needed to know that I could conquer them. Somehow, I was entwined with this path and it was here, between Mount Katahdin and Springer Mountain, that I hoped to realize exactly who and what I was, once and for all.

I pulled out my SPOT as I finished the chocolate and pushed the tracking button. Only a few people close to me had access to

it, so that strangers couldn't find me on the trail as they had on
the PCT. In fact, no one in the larger world would know what I
was doing until my scheduled Facebook announcement auto-
matically posted itself in three days. *By then I'll be almost through
the hundred-mile wilderness.*

I secured the beacon in the top pocket of my pack, took a deep
breath, and turned away from the summit sign. The fog lifted,
revealing the wilderness of Maine in each direction, and I began
following white blazes—descending Mount Katahdin on the
Appalachian Trail.

~

A few hours later I was deep in the forest of Baxter State Park.
My mind had settled, and I'd sunk into the rhythm of my own
body and breath. I was back on singletrack where I belonged. The
sound of a rushing creek reached my ears first and, when it came
into view, I was startled to find it wide and deep. I looked around
for a footbridge and then laughed at myself.

"Anish, you've been spoiled by the West."

I stepped into the water, finding it mildly amusing that I'd forgotten about the many deep fords in Maine. I wasn't even going
to make it to Abol Bridge at the south end of Baxter State Park
with dry feet. The creek was knee-deep and strong. I felt my feet
slide along the slippery rocks, fighting to find purchase. The liners in my shoes bunched up and slid under the balls of my feet.
I stepped out on the opposite bank, water streaming off of me,
and tried to straighten the liners, but they wouldn't stay in place.
They were determined to slide into a wrinkled bunch under the
arch of my foot. Impatient, I marched onward.

I exited the state park, turned right and walked the dirt road
across Abol Bridge. Shortly thereafter, I followed a white blaze
on a tree into the woods. Pleased to have reached my first mental waypoint since leaving Mount Katahdin, I managed to ignore

the uncomfortable inserts in my shoes as I tried to make up for the late—by FKT standards—start I'd had due to the wait at the entrance gate.

Crossing a slabby plateau in the late-afternoon sunshine, I glanced over my shoulder. Far in the distance, Mount Katahdin reigned benevolently. *It really is a beautiful mountain.* I descended back down into the woods along narrow tread. Every few hundred feet a four-by-two-inch white blaze reassured me I was on the correct path. I knew those rectangles would lead me inevitably to Springer Mountain in Georgia—if I didn't quit.

The mangled liners in my shoes were uncomfortable, and as my mileage for the day crested thirty, they became painful. I tried in vain to rearrange them several times, but they remained stubbornly wrinkled.

It was early evening when I passed an empty lean-to perched on the bluff above a rocky stream. Sitting on one large boulder in the middle was a ten-inch-high plastic T-Rex. I giggled at its incongruous presence as I dipped my bottle into the water and continued downstream, filtering through the attached Sawyer Squeeze while I walked. The Maine forest was thick, yet welcoming, and the humidity of the day eased as the light shifted from the sun's incandescence to softer shades of pearl. A silent eruption of shadows surged from the marshy land in front of me. I stopped in my tracks—unafraid, but curious. My brain decoded the confusion of light and gray to see the sleek lines of a great blue heron skimming across my field of vision. When it had disappeared, I breathed a deep sigh of contentment and quietly thanked it.

Later that evening, listening to the sound of a bullfrog lullaby echoing through the woods, I stretched my body out inside my tent. Every tendon, joint, and muscle from the hips down screamed at me. I'd managed well over forty miles, plus the additional five miles up Mount Katahdin to begin my thru-hike.

I could sense hot spots, formed by the bunching and rubbing inserts, pulsing on the arches and balls of my feet as I pulled my compression sleep socks on. I stretched the liners flat under my sleeping pad and hoped my weight and body heat would "iron" them overnight. After gulping down rehydrated refried beans—which would be my dinner nearly every night for all 2,189 miles—I clicked my headlamp off.

~

Two days later I dragged myself up the near vertical Fourth Chairback Mountain, gritting my teeth against the labor. Voluminous storm clouds were building once again into billowing towers far above the forested hills the AT climbed up and over. Despite my attempts, the shoe liners were beyond hope. No matter what I did, they bunched and slid from the near-constant rivers, puddles, and mud I hiked in and out of—except for times like this, when I scrambled up granite boulder fields, white blazes the only indication they formed part of the trail.

Finally, I reached the top and began to descend. I looked at the time: it was already afternoon and I needed to get to my resupply box—still twenty-five miles away—that day. Keeping to the pace I'd set for myself of nearly fifty miles per day felt like fighting a losing battle. I hadn't anticipated the toll the wetter than normal August would take on my feet.

My watch beeped, surprising me even though I'd just looked at it. It was time to eat. I pulled a baggie of dried goji berries out of my pocket and chewed them mechanically. From my experience on the PCT, I knew eating would be a struggle at the start of this endeavor. I also knew it was imperative to eat more protein, to not carry excess food weight, and to keep ingesting food no matter how little I wanted. My food plan took into account everything I'd learned on the PCT, as well as something crucial I'd learned ten months before starting the AT: I was allergic to gluten.

I swallowed the goji berries, full of protein and antioxidants, and shuddered, thinking about the diet of cookies, tortillas, crackers, and other wheat-based foods I'd lived on during my last long-distance FKT. I'd been poisoning myself with the very food meant to sustain me. Since finally getting a diagnosis, my ferritin levels had soared, my myriad vitamin deficiencies had resolved, and even my Raynaud's had improved dramatically. It seemed nothing short of miraculous.

"What better test of my newfound health than a 2,189-mile-long FKT," I teased myself, ruefully.

It was dusk when I reached the crossing of Highway 6; Monson, Maine, was eight miles eastward. I stopped to put my headlamp on at the trailhead and, after glancing at the sky, my poncho. The Appalachians do not mess around when it comes to precipitation. A jacket and poncho are required to stay even somewhat dry in their torrential downpours; however, it was too warm for both. No sooner had I crossed the road and followed the trail up the embankment than the first growls of thunder resounded. I hustled forward.

"Three miles. Left at the snowmobile trail. Half a mile. Left at the dirt road. On the left," I repeated the directions to the guide and outfitting business where my box was waiting for me.

Each time a bolt of lightning cracked the sky I jumped and hiked faster. The trail followed what seemed like an escarpment and, even though I was under the forest canopy, I felt closer to the angry sky than I would have expected. The wind picked up and the pines began to bend and dance. Flashes—both between the clouds and to the ground around me—came faster. I felt naked in the tempest as an icy torrent drenched me, wicking up from my dress hem and pouring down the collar of the poncho. The trail flooded and I floundered through the muddy water at top speed. My headlamp flickered and died, its electric arteries clogged by rainwater.

"No!" I cried, fumbling with cold, wet hands to turn on my second light. I secured it around my waist under the poncho, and aimed it at the ground. *Perhaps I should have worn the jacket.*

The storm was still raging as I followed the directions on the soggy sheet of paper torn from the guidebook. At last I found the darkened buildings of the outfitter and ran under one of their awnings. There, I pulled out my notes to see which building my box would be in after hours and began flashing my light at the signs over the porches, looking at the names.

"Who the hell are you?" a man's voice emanated from an adjacent building.

"Uh, hi, my name is Heather Anderson. I mailed a box here. I'm hiking the AT." I approached with my light lowered so he could see me. "I'm sorry it's so late. In your email you said it's in a building that I could just pick it up from. I really didn't mean to bother you."

"It's right here," he said, handing it to me.

"Thank you." I dug in my plastic bag wallet and pulled out five dollars. "Would it be ok if I empty it into my pack here? It's raining really hard and I need to get to the next shelter still. I'd rather not get everything wet while I transfer it."

He stared at me and the outstretched five. Silence reigned for a full thirty seconds. He made no move to take the money and no sound to answer my request. Finally, he spoke.

"The next shelter? You mean you're getting back on the trail? In this weather?" He trod through the questions slowly, as though they were incomprehensible.

"Yes, I have to keep hiking. That's why I sent the box here, so I wouldn't have to go into town."

I waved my hand slightly to remind him that my box fee was still awaiting collection. My arm was starting to tire from being outstretched. He looked down at the money, then back at my bedraggled visage.

"Put that away. You can't go back out in this!"

He waved his hand and I stuffed the bill back into its plastic baggie.

"Come with me."

I followed him through the rain over to the first building I'd run to, and he opened the door and flipped on the lights. It was a lounge with a picnic table, electric outlets, magazines, and maps. Best of all, it was heated.

"You can't go back out there in this," he repeated. "It's after ten o'clock. It's another five miles to the shelter. You can stay in here tonight."

"Oh, thank you, but I really need to keep hiking," I protested, even as temptation gripped my chilly, mud-covered body.

"No way. It's raining cats and dogs out there! Up in the small building with the light on is the bathhouse. Towels and everything you need are in there. Help yourself. I'll make you breakfast in the morning."

I didn't protest again. Laying my soaked gear out to dry, I thanked him again for his generosity and he bade me goodnight. It took all my remaining energy to drag myself to the hot shower, but as I snuggled into my sleeping bag with clean skin and hair, dry and safe from the storm, I knew that sacrificing five miles for a short walk to a shower and a dry place to sleep was worth it.

~

I was back on the Appalachian Trail by the time the sky turned lavender. The monstrous storm from the night before had subsided, leaving the tread a thick soup of squelching mud. I'd examined my feet before I put my shoes on that morning: The skin was badly chapped and chafed by the constant exposure to grit and water. Blisters had begun to form on the soles where the liner bunched and rubbed. Even though I'd rinsed my muddy socks in the shower and put on my clean pair this morning, I could still feel prickles of pain on the surface of my skin. To my despair, the clean socks had stayed clean approximately five feet down the trail.

Maybe I should throw the liners away? I thought for the thousandth time.

But each time I decided against it due to past experience. On my first AT thru-hike, I'd thrown out the inserts from my cheap shoes in Pennsylvania in an attempt to save weight. The result was such excruciating pain and blisters I'd had to throw the shoes themselves away. As a result, I ended up wearing a pair of shoes three sizes too big that I found in a hiker exchange box full of discarded items free for the taking.

"Ah!"

I nearly jumped out of my skin at the large, rattling animal lumbering across the trail ten feet from me. I squinted in the low light and was amazed to see a porcupine, the rattling sound emanating from the clanking of its elongated, hollow quills against the ground. It was a larger one than I'd ever seen before, and seemed unperturbed by my presence. Then again, if I wore extensive black-tipped body armor, I would not have been concerned with much either. I stood still, watching the porcupine amble into the bushes above the trail, and, still dragging its defenses, glance my way once before disappearing. I thought of the heron a few days before, and again, I was thankful.

The full morning light should have been on the banks of the West Branch of the Piscataquis River by the time I reached it. Instead, the sky was leaden and a fine mist was drifting down. I made my way to the heavily eroded, grassy bank and stopped to evaluate. I remembered it was a significant ford, but I was surprised to see how high it was after the deluge of the night before—not to mention the afternoon thunderstorms each of the last four days.

"This is new," I murmured, touching the cable, anchored to trees, that stretched across the wide expanse.

Although I forded this in the dark last time. Maybe it was there and I just didn't see it.

The water was colored cocoa by tannins and silt, but if the cable—hung several feet above my head—was any indication, it was not at flood stage. I lowered myself into the running water and let my feet settle into the silt and rocks. The cable was far out of reach above my head as water swooshed past my knees. I took a couple of careful steps once I was stable, using my trekking poles for balance.

Now that I was in the water, I could sense the river. "It will probably be waist deep or less in the middle," I reassured myself.

The water rose to my crotch as I moved my feet slowly over the slimy rocks, but I never felt like I was going to be knocked down. *Just don't step in a hole you can't see.* A few minutes later I was on the opposite bank, making my way back into the woods. My feet slipped and squelched in my shoes as the liners rolled and bunched. I could feel the hot spots growing worse, and looked down to see the red underside of the liner sticking out of the shoe near my ankle bone. *Like an impudent tongue stuck out at me.* Giving in to my frustration, I yanked it out and checked the other foot. Same. I stuffed them both into the side pocket of my pack and hiked on.

By the following afternoon my feet were killing me—with or without the liners, and whether I wore the mud-encrusted socks or the rinsed-but-still-dirty socks. I ignored the pain as I began the climb toward Middle and Pleasant Pond Mountains. The sun had disappeared behind a growing thunderstorm an hour before, and I looked up at the sky repeatedly. I knew a series of exposed slab traverses interspersed with stunted pines was in front of me—it was not a place I wanted to be in a thunderstorm. My watch beeped and I glanced at it: 2 p.m.

"I'm never going to make it at this pace," I said aloud.

The ferry across the Kennebec River stopped running at 5 p.m.—ten miles away over rugged terrain. I willed myself to move faster, even as I attempted to consume an energy bar. I choked on it and had to stop moving in order to finish eating. Then I took off again. In the distance I heard a rumble of thunder, spurring me to move even faster.

Running late seemed to be all I'd done since I'd left Millinocket. My start had been hindered by the lengthy line of cars waiting for the park gates to open. I'd failed to move as fast as I'd hoped in wet and muddy conditions. I'd met my mileage goal only once in my five days on trail—my first full one. Now, I was struggling to race not only a storm up a mountain, but also a canoe ferry at a river on the opposite side.

The air around me vibrated with anticipation. There was no doubt I was going to get walloped by the impending squall. I dropped my pack and whipped my poncho out, then put my pack back on and threw the poncho over my head as hail began to pummel me. With thunder shaking the sky and lightning blinding me, I comforted myself that—unlike on the ridgelines of the PCT—there was still a smattering of trees.

After twenty minutes I was growing impatient. The trees were shorter and less frequent. The hail had turned to a thick, gray curtain of heavy rain, making it difficult to spot the blazes painted on the slabs at my feet.

"Where is the top?"

I was soaked and the light and sound show around me gave no signs of relenting. Finally, after stopping more than once to evaluate whether I should duck down in the sparse trees and hide or keep hurrying forward, I reached a socked-in view and saw white blazes descending into the forest. I sped toward the longed-for cover and slipped and slid down the ottoman-sized rocks that formed the trail.

It quickly became clear that I would have to pay close attention to the blazes on the trees as I raced to the Kennebec. The "trail" was comprised of blocky rocks, exposed roots, and a whole lot of deep, sucking mud pits. The monsoon had turned the entire mountainside into rivulets and cascades that made the AT indistinguishable from a creek. After my third fall on the rocks, I simply sat in the water while I composed myself. I looked at my watch. 3:45 p.m.

"I'm going to miss the ferry today."

It was a bitter blow after everything I'd done to get myself there. Blood was running down my leg from where I'd cut it on the rocks during one of my falls. Tears of frustration ran down my cheeks. I'd done nothing but hemorrhage time since the moment I started my tracking beacon. *I really am incapable.* There was no way I could repeat the success of the PCT. I was less than a week in, and I was already failing.

"Get up," I ordered myself.

At a safer pace, I continued down the mountain. The rain slowed as the storm faded away. I was not going to make the ferry today, but I knew that—realistically—it probably wouldn't have been operating during the storm anyway. Still, I was angry at myself for staying at the outfitter rather than putting in the extra mileage. *You'll never make it if you are that weak-willed!* Perhaps those few miles would have made the difference. I was also irritated at where an unfordable river was placed in my schedule. But mostly, I was upset with the weather.

"I know it rains a lot here, but seriously?"

"Hey! Are you a southbounder?"

I started at the sound of a man's voice: in front of me stood another thru-hiker. He looked relatively clean and I assumed he was a northbounder who had just departed the hostel in Caratunk a short distance off trail on this side of the Kennebec.

"Uh, yeah."

"Oh man. Man, this river is crazy. It's not safe to cross, not at the trail. There's a log. It's high. I mean, I scooched and my feet were almost in the water. Shit. It's bad. It's upstream."

He rampaged through words in an adrenaline-fueled frenzy. Glancing to my left, I realized I'd been so lost in my own thoughts I hadn't noticed the roaring of Holly Brook. I felt a constriction in my gut. All the water racing past me down Pleasant Pond Mountain funneled into this drainage.

"Oh." I turned back to him. "Log upstream to cross on. Ok. Thank you."

"Sure," he said, then paused. "Let me show you."

"That's not necessary."

My words were in vain since he was already booking it back down the trail in the direction he had come. I shifted back into gear and took off after him at four miles per hour down the wide, slightly declined trail. He was still talking about the river, the log, and how scary it had been, but I only caught a few words over the roar of the brook. We came to a halt about a quarter of a mile later next to some flattened vegetation where it was obvious someone had trampled from the river to the trail.

"It's right in there," he said, pointing.

I looked in the direction of the river fifteen feet away and saw part of a thick tree extending over it. The rest was obscured by the brush and plants crowding the bank.

"Thank you." I reiterated my appreciation, expecting him to take off at the same rapid pace with which he'd brought me to the tree. Instead he stood there expectantly.

Resigned, I turned and started picking my way through the damaged flora toward the log across Holly Brook. I reached the upended root ball and turned to see my guide still standing on the trail, watching. With a small wave, I started climbing up the exposed roots to reach the trunk. The brook stampeded under the tree at a dizzying speed. I'd initially been miffed that my escort had essentially denied me a chance to go to the trail cross-ing and make my own decision about whether to ford or cross a suspended tree. But, watching the movement of the water, I real-ized I'd have made the same decision and he had indeed saved me a half mile of walking back and forth. Clambering over the top of the roots, I stepped down onto the rough, wet bark. I scuffed my shoe across the log a couple of times to assess the grip. It was a good twenty feet across and I didn't particularly want to butt scoot that far unless absolutely necessary.

"Good enough."

As I started my tightrope walk above the raging brown water, I focused on my feet, the feel of the tree, and my breath—balancing on high logs requires focus. Safely on the opposite bank, I looked back and saw the hiker's tan shirt and gray pack disappearing northbound up the trail. I began making my way downriver, but the embankment was softened by the precipitation and contin-ually slid out from under me. Ascending to firmer ground fifteen feet above the river, I fought my way through saplings and hip-deep greenery that caught at my dress and shoelaces. But after ten minutes I felt slightly panicked. *I should be back on the trail by now.*

I yanked my phone out and waited for the Guthook app to assess my location. To my relief, the trail was only ten more feet downriver. I angled upward, and intersected it at the top of the embankment. Seeing a white blaze on a prominent tree, I pock-eted the phone and laughed at myself.

"Who knew I'd end up bushwhacking down a flooded river looking for the 'best marked trail in the world'?"

The rain had stopped completely by the time I reached the highway crossing. I paused briefly to look for traffic on the seldom-used road before bolting across and into a gap in the trees marked by a white blaze on the other side. A pickup was parked in the pullout alongside the trail—my heart soared.

Maybe the ferry operator is still here! It was 6 p.m., but renewed hope made my legs move faster and I jogged the half mile to the Kennebec River crossing. It was abandoned.

Dejected, I walked to the water's edge and gazed at the 400-foot-wide river. It was likely chest-deep on me, and it flowed quietly, unfazed by the torrents of fresh rainfall that had so recently merged with it. I prodded the water's edge with my trekking pole and thought about swimming across. Jennifer Pharr Davis had forded this river during her supported FKT four years prior—as had many people over the years, despite the huge sign hanging behind me warning about rapidly fluctuating river levels. A dam upstream could cause the river to rise four or more feet without warning. Squinting, I tried to assess how deep it was now. I thought about Jennifer's lanky frame and her additional five inches of height compared to mine. I also thought about my intense fear of the water and the many anxiety attacks I'd experienced in flatwater, while snorkeling, and in small boats.

"I'm going to have to wait," I said to the river.

I turned around and inspected the cherry-red canoe beached a few feet away. I lifted it and looked for paddles. There were none, but the familiar white blaze smiled at me from where it was painted on the bottom of the boat. I set it back down.

"The boat *is* the official trail, after all."

I wandered over to the privy perched on a platform and scouted for paddles there too. After abandoning my search efforts, I hiked back up the trail to find a place to spend the next fifteen hours. I knew that even if I'd found the paddles I wouldn't have taken the boat, but it had made me feel somewhat better to check. I pulled the pages of my guidebook out of my dress pocket and looked at the options in Caratunk back at the road crossing. There was a hostel and restaurant, if I wanted to walk some

bonus miles there and back. I realized I was crying with frustration. I really didn't want to add extra miles and I certainly didn't
want to see anyone. I shoved the pages back into my pocket and
stared at the forest. *I could just go there and hitch out. Give up. So
many setbacks in just a few days . . . I'm so far off schedule and this
just makes it worse.*

Sunshine percolated through the conifer boughs, dappling
the droplet-covered terrain with shimmering light. In the back-
ground I could hear the purr of the river—content to go wherever
gravity pulled it. I sighed and wandered around in the woods until
I found a suitable campsite. After pitching my tent, I crawled in
and jotted down my mileage for the day on my spreadsheet before
eating dinner. Then I lay back—staring at the patterns of light
and shadow dancing on the translucent fabric of my tent. Unlike
the river, I was far from content. I was resigned. I was nowhere
near my goal of fifty miles per day. And now I was sitting on a
riverbank on a sunny evening when I should have been cruising
along the mellow terrain south of here. But the greatest lessons
from setting an FKT on the PCT had been about mindfulness and
acceptance. Over those long, dusty miles I'd found peace in the
knowledge that I couldn't control the wildness around me, but
instead learned to become part of it—accepting what it was and
wasn't. I closed my eyes and focused on those lessons instead of
an uncrossable river flowing by.

Over the years my parents had planted three groves of coni-
fers on their twenty-eight acres of mostly hardwood forest. Now,
mature, neatly organized stands of blue spruce and white pine
patchwork the landscape. They remain unwavering dark green
as the seasons in the deciduous trees around them progress from
bright emerald to the messy riot of autumnal colors and, finally,
winter's dull gray. As a child I used to press my nose into a soft
bough of needles and inhale deeply—the refreshing aroma stood

out from the earthy humus scent of the woods around them. In the fall, the groves were quiet, restful chapels in contrast to the loudly crunching woodland paths. Yet, when I first moved to the Evergreen State every small clutch of aspen made my soul swim with nostalgia and love for the changing seasons. Colored foliage there was few and far between. In a land of never-ending pines, leaves didn't crackle under my feet. Every October I longed for the Midwest.

I supposed it was human nature to want what we do not have. I wanted to be across the river and making progress toward my goal. Instead I was lying in a coppice of both pine and deciduous trees, reminiscent of my two homes. And, like it or not, this place would be home for the next fifteen hours. I could waste mental energy fighting it or accept the reality with as much grace as I could muster. Taking a deep breath, I inhaled the scent of pine needles and dark earth.

I sighed and rolled over. I wondered what was happening back in the forests of Michigan. I wondered how my mother's therapy was progressing. I hadn't called home. I wouldn't until I was done. There wasn't really time, and I knew it could cause me to lose focus. My sister was receiving my SPOT pings and she'd contact me if there was an emergency. *Will Mom talk again?* I wondered.

My thoughts wandered to my old camera, the one I'd used before I'd gotten a smartphone. The shutter didn't close correctly, and the zoom had been pathetic. I remembered how upset I was that it could never capture the moment. Until one evening, as sunset caught my world on fire, I found the silver lining. It was then that I learned not to squander fleeting moments clicking through settings and framing an angle. Instead, I spent them fully focused on the experience. Getting rid of my camera taught me to drink in the vistas, the sunsets, the chance wildlife encounters with my whole being and my whole mind.

I'd encountered a crane, a porcupine, and moose in the first four days of this hike, yet I had no pictures of them. The images in my mind were crystal clear and that was enough. I lay still, listening to the forest's small sounds and feeling the soft—yet solid—earth cradling my tired body. Golden light from the sinking sun illuminated my tent. With complete awareness of the oasis I'd inadvertently found, I fell fast asleep.

The sun was still merrily dancing across the fabric of my tent when I opened my eyes. I was initially confused—the angle of the light seemed abruptly different. *It's morning!* I sat up with sudden urgency and found my watch at the foot of the tent.

"Eight. Thank God."

I quickly ate breakfast and packed my things. Twenty minutes later, I popped out of the tent, still surprised I'd slept soundly for nearly fourteen hours. I was grateful for the respite—for the first time since starting the hike I hadn't woken up feeling battered or groggy.

I was back at the canoe at a quarter to nine, relieved that no other hikers had arrived and lined up ahead of me. The ferry was a slow process, with no more than two hikers crossing at a time. I was determined to be first in line.

"Good mornin'." A bearded man carrying several paddles emerged from the trees.

"Hi. I'm glad to see you! I've been waiting since yesterday."

"Yep," he said, bustling around getting life vests out of a barrel and flipping the canoe. He dragged it to the water's edge and looked across, shading his eyes with one hand.

"Looks like they were too."

I looked over and noticed the forms of several people on the opposite bank. He handed me a clipboard and a liability waiver. I filled it in.

"Had to get off the water at one thirty yesterday cause of the lightnin'. S'prised there aren't more of ya' stacked up."

I exchanged the form for a life vest and put it on. He put my pack in the boat and I awkwardly shimmied to the bow. He handed me a paddle.

"Now you get to do some of the work. You just paddle on that side and leave the rest to me," he said, pointing upriver.

"Cross-training," I quipped. He smiled and pushed us into the current.

I couldn't see the bottom through the murky water and, even though I was doing a fraction of the work, I could tell the ferry operator was pushing hard to maneuver us upriver into the current. From there, we could turn to ride it downstream and out again—gliding gently into a reedy landing. I felt my stomach clench at the idea of attempting to swim it. The canoe bumped the embankment and brought my eyes up to the grass and mud. I clambered out and unfastened my life vest.

"Alrighty, have a good 'un." He handed me my pack and turned to the waiting hikers with his clipboard.

I sped down the trail as though I'd been shot from a catapult. Rest, combined with a sense of urgency due to lost time, sent me scurrying over wet rocks and ploughing through the mud as fast as I could go. The terrain was mellow, enabling me to move at a consistent pace, something the rocky, rooty AT seldom allowed. By midafternoon I had slowed somewhat, having blown through the initial reserves of energy stored up by the extra hours of rest. When I stopped for water at a gushing stream, I set my Sawyer filter to gravity flow and quickly pulled my mud-caked shoes off of my feet. I swished my socks in the runnel and wrung out brown liquid onto the ground away from the stream. I rinsed and repeated the process a couple more times.

"That should help at least." I flipped my pack over to unfasten the ones that had been drying on the loops since the morning before and swap them with the freshly rinsed ones.

There were no socks.

"Oh my God."

I quickly pulled everything out of my backpack. It was true. There was only one pair of hiking socks. I realized with dismay that the shrubs I'd waded through after the log crossing of Holly Brook must have snatched them off my pack. I stared at the muddy shoes, wet socks, and my chafed, blistered feet. With only one pair of socks I would not be able to give my feet a break from the ingrained dirt that rubbed them constantly. I reached into my dry bag and pulled out my knee-high compression socks. They were what I wore to sleep in—for recovery and to keep my sleeping bag clean. I shoved them back into the dry bag.

"I'll just have to deal with it."

MUD, ROCKS,
AND BLOOD

AS IS OFTEN THE case when living in nature, I began to lose track of time. Miles went by in a haze of mud, roots, and rocks, interspersed by trees speckled with white blazes. I dutifully added the day's mileage to my spreadsheet every night, aware that I was falling further and further behind my projected pace. Two miles here, four miles there . . . it all amounted to a great heap of failure in my mind. In the rocky, mountainous center of Maine, I fought to try and eke out every mile in my plan, but I was incapable of moving faster than two miles per hour. I would wake at four in the morning and hike until ten at night, all to hit my goal of hiking the trail in fifty days—or less. That was faster than I needed to go for a self-supported FKT, but I wanted to come as close as I could to the supported times held by Jennifer Pharr Davis and Scott Jurek.

I didn't want to break Matt Kirk's fifty-eight-day self-supported record by a few hours. I didn't need to set just another self-supported record—I needed to set a decisive one. I needed to know I was capable. That I wasn't a failure. That the JMT attempt had been the fluke, not my PCT hike. I needed to crush the self-doubt once and for all. Yet, less than a week into my journey I was already more than a day behind my aggressive schedule.

Thunder roared overhead as it did every afternoon. I gave it a cursory glance up through the trees, and then looked back down at the spring I'd just reached. While filling my bottle I looked at the Guthook navigation app on my phone to see how far the next spring was.

Boxed spring. On the summit of Bigelow. Shouldn't need a lot then. I put the lid back on my bottle and trucked through the rain.

I began to ascend the next mountain range as the cloudburst ended. The climb seemed to take an eternity. With the humidity soaring I guzzled my water, finishing it before I reached the top of Little Bigelow. I made my way along a ridgeline that alternated between open views and forest, my shoes sliding on the wet rock slabs. The sun sank ever closer to the horizon, silhouetting the distant mass of Bigelow's highest summit, Avery Peak, against the lavender sky.

At dusk I crested it, drinking in the view of swaths of forested mountains rolling in all directions, and began searching for the spring. I found the small wooden box and yanked the lid open. A small puddle greeted me.

I stuck my bottle in and tried to scoop the water, but was only successful in gathering a sip. The horizon was now devoid of its ball of fire, so I grabbed my headlamp out of my pack, scooped another sip from the spring, and, despite my thirst, slammed the lid shut. With all the rain I'd expected more water.

"I've got to move," I said to myself.

I flew along the slabby ridgeline and found the blaze marking the descent. Gloom overtook the trail as soon as I plunged under tree cover and lost most of the remaining light. Every day

I eschewed turning on my headlamp until it was pitch black. It was a game I enjoyed playing: "How deep into the twilight can your eyes see?" Dimly, a few dozen feet ahead of me, I made out a hulking form on the trail. Realizing I was not alone in the game of night, I skidded to a halt. It took a mere split second for me to realize it was a moose—and that it had a calf.

"Aah!" I backpedaled at top speed until I was fifty feet away.

Breathing heavily with shaking hands, I fumbled to turn on my headlamp while keeping a lookout for rampaging *Cervidae*. Once it was on, I crept forward slowly, making as much racket as I would for a bear. Maybe even more noise, as I'd seen video of a mama moose kicking a grizzly to death in defense of her calf. After a few feet I saw them loitering in the middle of the trail. I peeled off and headed straight up the hillside—crashing through herbage, pine saplings, and deadfall. I was making so much noise I couldn't tell if the two moose were following me or not. After fifty vertical feet and a hundred horizontal I began angling back, stumbling back onto the AT fifteen minutes after initially spotting the moose. I shined my light northbound and saw nothing— then I heard a grunt. With that warning, I fled southbound.

Once I felt safe, I pulled out my phone and checked Guthook. Eventually, I'd be following a creek downhill. *I'll have water soon.* Turning off the phone, I continued hiking. I'd barely begun, and Maine was crushing me.

~

In the morning, I grabbed my headlamp and crawled out of my tent. It was only 4:15 a.m., but the sky was already graying. With the long days, I needed my headlamp only to break down camp and for an hour or so at night, nothing more. Outside the vestibule, my light caught a gleaming stain on the leaves. I aimed the beam directly at it and stared: blood.

I glanced around the campsite. The forest was quiet—save for the normal rustling that marked the changing of the guard from nocturnal to diurnal. Unnerved, I packed quickly and headed down the trail. *Why was there blood outside my tent?*

As I neared Maine Route 27, I stopped and hiked up my skirt to pee. The stream was the color of Merlot.

"Oh my God."

I realized suddenly that the blood on the ground outside the tent was where I'd peed overnight. In the dark I hadn't seen the color, but now in broad daylight it was obvious.

"I'm peeing blood."

I finished urinating and stood still for a moment. My heart raced and my mind—wild and frantic—ran in myriad directions all at once. I tried to focus on my body, taking several slow, deep breaths.

"I don't have a fever," I said, palpating my abdomen. "No tenderness. No pain when urinating."

I started walking slowly, calming myself as I mulled over the symptoms. After crossing the empty road, I began the ascent to the Crocker Mountains—that traverse would be followed by the Saddleback Range. Today would have 10,000 feet of gain over forty-odd miles. It was not a good day to be bleeding internally.

"Not that there's ever a good day to bleed internally," I said, grimacing, and started upward.

Hours later I was still peeing burgundy. It was so dark I had trouble believing there was even urine mixed in. I'd decided that the only thing I could do was attempt to clear whatever was happening from my system with copious amounts of fluid, so I increased my water intake twofold. Although I didn't have any other symptoms, I knew it could be serious and that, if it didn't stop, I would have to seek medical attention. Up and down the rocky, slippery mountains, I forced myself to drink, stopping to pee every thirty minutes. Each time I held my breath and bit my lip, hoping to see signs of improvement. There were none. By midday I felt tenderness and cramping in my abdomen. I chugged water. Still I peed Merlot.

"The discomfort is probably because of the increased urination," I told myself as the temperature and humidity soared. But in my head I was less optimistic. *This is it. This is the last setback. One I can't overcome.*

As I made my way up the steep grade of Saddleback Mountain I began running into northbound hikers. Most were listening to headphones and merely nodded at the sight of me. One man stopped and greeted me, "Hey! How're you?"

"Not great. I'm peeing blood." I'd lost all hope and illusion of strength.

He paused. "I'm sorry. That's rough. I think there's a clinic in Rangeley. Or maybe someone will have some antibiotics?"

"Thanks."

I sank onto a fallen log as he disappeared down the trail. My abdomen cramped and I hunched over, holding my hips and clenching my teeth. I felt tears hit my bare knees and forearms. *This isn't fair! I've hardly begun and it's already over. I failed before I even got out of Maine! What is going on? This is hardly the most difficult thing I've done. Did I break myself on the JMT? Am I dying?*

Another hiker came by.

"Are you ok?"

"Yes," I lied.

"Sure?"

"Yeah, just taking a break."

I looked up and forced a smile. He nodded and walked off. I reeled my mind in and started climbing again. When I finally broke tree line I was met with brilliant sunshine and clear skies.

For the first afternoon of my trip, no storm clouds threatened. I climbed to the top of Saddleback Mountain and crouched down to check my phone. I had texted my boyfriend earlier asking him to look up possible reasons why I might be peeing blood. Pulling out my phone, I was relieved to see I had service. *Maybe he's replied.* I opened Google Maps and looked for the clinic in Rangeley. It would add sixteen miles roundtrip if I were to walk in from where the AT crossed the upcoming highway. I'd essentially lose an entire day. *But is it worth losing an entire thru-hike and maybe the record? Screw the record, is it worth dying? I should just quit in Rangeley . . . and see the doctor.*

My phone pinged. My boyfriend's text read, "You could have Exercise-Induced Hematuria. Basically, bladder rub if you were dehydrated for a long time while hiking or running." I skimmed the description he sent me. I hadn't been without water for very long while crossing the Bigelows. But it was a benign option indicating no long-term health damage so I decided to cling to it. I closed my phone, gulped some water, and hiked on.

The sun skimmed the tops of the trees as I finally reached the lowlands south of the Saddlebacks. I was not far from a privately owned and operated hostel called the Hiker Hut, and my second resupply of the hike. I mentally prepared myself to go in, grab my box, and get out. It would be after seven o'clock when I arrived—I'd moved slower than I'd wanted to that day. My abdomen remained tender. *Should I go to Rangeley?* I knew I didn't have another eight miles in me to reach town. *Should I stay at the Hut and go into Rangeley tomorrow?* I glimpsed a car pass by on the highway, barely visible through the trees. I turned to the side of the trail and lifted my skirt.

"It's clear!"

After an entire day of hoping, I was shocked to see urine free of blood.

"Thank God," I murmured to myself as I sped toward the road. I turned into the driveway of the Hiker Hut and, following a sign's instructions, pulled a rope attached to an enormous bell. Its gong announced my presence to the proprietor and about a dozen people who were gathered around a campfire beside several buildings. They cheered and waved a welcome. I collapsed into an offered chair by the fire, relieved in many ways. Steve, the owner, brought over my box and offered me a place to stay.

"It's twenty-five dollars for dinner, breakfast, and a bunk."

"Oh, no thank you. I need to do a few more miles tonight. I just want to go through my box." Now that I was no longer bleeding, I couldn't justify another unplanned stay.

"Ok, well let me know if you need anything. Make yourself at home." Steve disappeared into one of the cabins.

My mouth watered at the sight of the delicious buffet set out nearby, but I reminded myself that I had a budget and a schedule. I ripped open my box and pulled out a precooked pouch of Indian food. Paneer is not very palatable without reheating, but it offered calories and a savory break from the mostly sweet snack foods I had been consuming on trail. I sucked it down rapidly while simultaneously yanking trash out of my pack and throwing my newly acquired rations—2,500 calories a day—into my food bag. *Efficiency* repeated in my mind constantly, alternating with *You're behind schedule.*

I glanced up at the woman who was sitting in the chair beside me. She had brown hair, appeared to be in her late forties, and was observing me with interest. I became aware of the Indian food smeared on my chin and my animal-like freneticism.

"Are you southbound or northbound?" a guy on my other side asked.

"Sobo," I replied, wiping my face with the back of my hand and composing myself.

"When did you start?"

"August 1." My attempt at civility was short-lived. I opened a packet of dried seaweed and stuffed all twenty-five squares into my mouth.

"Holy shit." He was openly staring—whether at my gross feeding habits or my mileage, I wasn't sure. Probably both.

"That's like, forty miles a day!" another hiker observed.

I nodded.

"What are you trying to do? Set a record?" the first guy asked.

"Yes," I said quietly.

The brown-haired woman sitting beside me got up and went over to Steve. The other hikers began bombarding me with questions.

"How fast are you trying to go?"

"How?"

"Why would you do that?"

"I'm trying to hike it in about fifty days," I answered. "As close to the supported time of forty-six days as I can get—self-supported. I don't have a crew. I just walk long hours every day. After I set the self-supported record on the Pacific Crest Trail two years ago, it made me curious what I could do out here. I hiked the AT twelve years ago—I've missed it."

The woman returned and sat down as I finished my answers. I looked at her and opened my mouth to apologize for my initial disgusting behavior, but instead I blurted out, "Are you from Seattle?"

She glanced down at her sweatshirt, where the city name was printed in block letters.

"Yes, I am. Although originally from out here. Steve's my brother and I'm visiting. I've lived in Seattle for almost thirty years."

I felt a pang of homesickness. The day had been draining, and I was still scared about what had happened inside my body. Alone, I felt the enormity of what I had yet to do. I wanted a friend. Someone to hug me and tell me it was going to be ok.

"I'm Sue," she said, smiling.

"Anish." I smiled back. Sue had given me the friendly reassurance I needed simply with her presence.

"Welcome to the Hut, Anish. We're so honored to have you."

"Thank you." I looked around at the hikers eating, drinking, and laughing. I suddenly had the desire to stay a week and forget the FKT. "What do you do in Seattle?"

"Oh, I'm a nurse."

My head snapped back to her so fast it surprised even me. She lifted her eyebrows slightly.

"Can I ask you a question? I mean, I know nurses and doctors hate people asking for medical advice all the time and I'm sorry. I'm just really desperate."

"Sure."

"I've been peeing really dark blood for twenty-four hours. I don't have a fever or pain or burning. I mean I have discomfort in my abdomen, but it could be from the sheer volume of liquids I processed today—I forced myself to drink two gallons of water. I know there's a clinic in Rangeley, but since I'm doing a self-supported record I would have to walk there and back. The last time I urinated, about twenty minutes before I got here, it was clear. I thought I might have runner's bladder rub."

She thought for a minute.

"Well, blood in the urine can be very serious, and you really should be checked out at a clinic. It could be stones, infection, or dehydration, but with the bleeding you describe, there is a risk of renal failure. You're sure your urine is clear now and you have no other symptoms?"

I reassured her that my bleeding had stopped and I had no other symptoms.

Sue continued, "My father was a world-class athlete and Steve was too. I know you guys push your limits for the sake of your sport. You are probably right in your diagnosis. You have to promise me you'll stay hydrated and be seen by a doctor if your bleeding persists, or you develop other symptoms."

"I promise. Thanks for listening."

"Absolutely."

Steve strolled over.

"Hey, Anish, Sue told me that you're trying for the record. That's so cool! Please, help yourself to food."

"Oh, thank you, but that's ok. I really should keep going."

"It's already dark."

"I know, I just didn't budget for staying, unless maybe there's a spot I can tent for less?"

"No, it's all twenty-five dollars."

"Ok, I understand. Is there a trash can for my box?"

"You can break it down right over there and we'll use it to start fires. The can for trash is beside it."

"Thanks."

I headed over to the trash and started to break apart my box. Steve followed me.

"Hey, you can stay for free. No worries. I want to support your record. Sue even said you can sleep with her in the canvas tent by the river. It's quiet. Best place on the property," he offered quietly so others didn't hear.

"Oh. Thank you so much. I can't accept though. I have a rule for this hike: I won't accept special treatment because of what I'm trying to do."

"I insist."

He walked away and I realized, just like in Monson, it was pointless to argue. *Mainers. Won't take no for an answer,* I giggled to myself. I went over to the buffet and heaped a plate full of homemade food. After all, I was drained and I *wanted* to stay. Rejoining Sue at the campfire, we talked until I couldn't keep my eyes open. She led me to her platform canvas tent, and I crawled into my bag.

"I'm sorry, my alarm will go off at 4 a.m."

"I don't mind a bit. I'll go right back to sleep."

As I dozed off, I thought about how grateful I was to not have to set up my tent. When my alarm went off, six hours later, I awoke confused as to where I was.

"Sue," I whispered, realizing I had a tentmate.

I pounced on my alarm, silencing it as quickly as I could. She rolled over and murmured, "Good luck, Anish."

"Thank you," I whispered back. *Thank you for giving me the courage to keep going and not quit.*

I shoved my sleeping bag into my pack and put my headlamp on. Then I pulled twenty-five dollars out of my wallet and laid it on the pillow. Tearing off a scrap from my guidebook page, I used my pencil to write, "Thank you Sue and Steve." Having tucked it under the corner of the bills, I trudged outside into the pitch black.

~

"Maine is ridiculously hard." Leaning against a tree, I tilted my head forward and looked at my bare feet. Without a second pair of hiking socks, they were hopelessly destroyed. Each was speckled with red, blotchy chafe. Huge blisters encompassed the arches, balls of the foot, and heels, thanks to the constant wetness and sliding around in my shoes. I'd just spent forty minutes scrambling and squeezing through the infamous boulder patch called Mahoosuc Notch. Ahead of me lay six miles of up and down through alpine bogs and over ledgy summits—to the New Hampshire border.

"And New Hampshire won't be any better," I sighed. "I don't know how I will walk another 1,900 miles like this. I feel like giving up."

I sent my eyes upward, away from my battered feet, into the gently swaying boughs far above my head. *I was a climber of trees before I became a climber of mountains.* Every time I gazed upward into towering branches, I thought about my roots. This moment was no different. Beginnings, paths, and cycles were on my mind nonstop during this hike. I was not certain how it was going to end, but I could apperceive all the journeys I'd ever taken providing an anchor within me like the taproot of a venerable oak. An anchor that assured me I would find my way back to myself—and to whatever I was seeking out here in the rocks and mud.

In my mind, I was seven again, sitting in a young silver maple, fifteen feet above the emerald lawn. The air was thick with water vapor, as it always is during a Midwestern summer. I was intrigued by the emptiness below my bare feet as they swung on either side of a branch. I could see about a mile away before a line of trees broke the agricultural monotony. What would it be like to be in one of those trees? *I wondered.* How far could I see from there? What could I see? How far could I walk in a day if I started early? If that's all I did? Could I make it to Lansing where Dad worked? He drove back and forth five days a week, so maybe . . . ? *It seemed so impossibly far away: forty-five miles.*

I heard the back door bang open and my mom shout for me. I didn't move; she'd check here eventually. She had learned that whenever Heather went missing all she had to do was look up. I loved the feeling of space under my feet and the way the world looked from up high. There was nothing I couldn't—and wouldn't—climb.

"HEATHER!"

I looked down to see my mom in miniature. The way height changed her size and shape was fascinating. She looked flattened somehow.

"It's time for lunch. Get down here. I'm afraid you're going to hurt yourself!"

I swung off of the branch I'd been sitting on and started climbing down. At the last branch, I did a forward flip, landing in the grass beside my mom. My feet slipped out and I fell onto my butt.

My mom sighed and pulled me to my feet. For the first few years of my life she'd tried to put me in frilly dresses. By the time I was mobile she could see that though I might not genetically be the son she'd wanted, I was going to be one hell of a tomboy. When I turned three she gave up and went to the farm store to buy a pair of boy's denim overalls.

We walked hand in hand to the house, with me only half hearing her admonitions about grass stains and tree climbing. I went into the bathroom to wash up, continuing to muse. How far could I walk in a day if that's all I did? How many hours could I walk before I got tired? What about lunch? *Cold well water rinsed a steady stream of dirt down the drain.* Would I wrap my food in a bandanna and hang it on a stick over my shoulder like I saw in the cartoons? I don't know how to do that. Maybe mom would help.

My stomach growled. I shut off the water and headed for the dining room.

~

Under the tree, my stomach alerted me to my hunger, pulling me from my reverie. My mom had never quite understood my need for the wild. But she had been the one to pack and mail me every resupply box on my first three thru-hikes. The food was not wrapped in a bandanna, but it was wrapped in copious bubble wrap and always included a letter of love and support.

Leaning forward, I heaved myself up and took a few hobbling steps. My feet recoiled from the return to their relentless excoriation, but soon my stride evened out. Once again, I was sloshing through liquefied mud while munching on a granola bar.

Hours later, without daylight, I strained to follow a trail that had become nothing but piles of rocks covered in trees. It couldn't be more than a mile to the New Hampshire border. I stomped in frustration despite the agony the tantrum sent jolting through my feet. I could not find the trail in the rocks.

"Screw you, Maine!" I got onto my hands and knees and began examining the boulders with my headlamp.

Soon, I found small white scratches on the surface of one boulder and inspected the one above. I found more.

Trekking pole marks.

I followed the white scratches—passing a long-lost pink Nalgene—up the hill until I lost the trail yet again. I hadn't intended to stop for the night until I reached New Hampshire . . . maybe even Mount Success a few miles beyond the border. Yet at the pace I was moving I would be lucky to reach my goal before sunrise. I was also utterly spent.

"Home for the night, I guess," I muttered as I stretched out on the trail, thankful that—for once—it wasn't a slop of mud.

LETTING GO

THE DIFFICULTY OF THE dark hours seemed distant as I neared the summit of Mount Success—as did my mysterious hematuria. Though the internal bleeding was now only a memory, I sometimes still anxiously held my breath when I stopped to pee.

Sun stippled the forest and I relished the chirping of birds—the only sound aside from my own footfalls on the relatively dry trail. I felt the light melting away my melancholy. In fourteen miles I would reach Highway 2, where I could pick up ice cream—at least according to the comments in the Guthook app and Awol guide. And in twenty-four hours I would be in Pinkham Notch picking up a resupply box that contained new shoes and socks. My feet craved the cushion and unsoiled fibers. I would be fighting class three technical trail and talus until I reached Vermont, over 150 miles distant. But I also knew there'd be less mud. For that I was grateful.

CRACK!

I stopped, startled at the sound of breaking branches and pounding of massive hooves. I looked to my right in time to see a huge bull moose disappearing into the forest at full speed, its hurtling mass decimating the silence as it cleaved a path through thick woodland litter. Relieved to see he was heading away from me, I increased the distance between us as fast as I could.

A few hours later the trail merged with a dirt road. My pace naturally increased on the even tread and pleasant grade as I descended toward the Androscoggin River. Occasionally a car passed me, its occupants offering the casual waves common to rural life. Soon I was on the lawn of the Rattle River Hostel, a huge white house that had been converted to hiker lodging. I filled my water bottles from the outside spigot, then quickly rinsed out my squalid, tattered socks before putting them back on and lacing up my filthy shoes. I went into the garage and listened politely as the hiker there told me how the hostel worked.

When he concluded I asked, "Can I buy some ice cream?"

"Uh, yeah, it's inside in the kitchen. You put your money in the can next to the fridge."

"I'm actually not staying. Can I just give you the money to grab me one?"

His speech had included an entire set of instructions about hikers not going into the house in their shoes or socks. My tender, blistered feet were not in the mood to have their socks and shoes removed and replaced any more than necessary. He stared at me slightly confused and then nodded.

"Thanks so much."

I handed him the money and he disappeared into the kitchen. I heard the freezer door open.

"What flavor do you want? Cookie dough, Cherry Garcia, or peanut butter cup?"

"The peanut butter cup."

He returned with the ice cream. "Here ya' go."

"Thank you!"

"You're really not staying?"

"No, I need to get to Pinkham Notch tomorrow."

I could feel his stare on me until I was out of the garage.

I tossed the empty ice cream container into the trash at the trailhead a quarter mile down the highway. The influx of sugar into my bloodstream had energized me. A few feet away was a cooler of trail magic that looked as if it had been there for months. I pried the lid open, expecting to find it empty. Instead there was an entire package of gluten-free sandwich cookies. When I pulled them out, I saw they'd expired two months before. I shrugged and shoved them into my pack: I was down to one dinner and three bars. The ice cream, and now the cookies, were a boon that would fuel me for the twenty-one miles to Pinkham Notch. I was standing at about 700 feet above sea level. Over the next seven miles, I would hike upstream along the Rattle River before climbing to the summit of Mount Moriah at over 4,000 feet. In the miles following that ascent were the ups and downs over North, Middle, and South Carter Mountains, as well as Mount Hight and Carter Dome—all in quick succession—before the AT plummeted down to 3,200 feet at the Carter Notch Hut. Then I'd climb back up to 4,400-foot-high Wildcat Mountain, where I planned to camp.

Several hours after I had left the trailhead, I sat at Zeta Pass in the midst of the Carters, filtering water. Mount Hight and Carter Dome loomed 1,000 feet above me. My feet ached. I was only three trail miles from Wildcat Mountain, but the combined elevation change and the steep, rocky scrambling meant it would take me at least two hours to get there, especially since it was already dusk. Hearing voices, I looked up to see three men in their fifties coming toward me from up the trail.

"Hello."

"Hi," one of them greeted me as they sat down on the ground and promptly began prepping camp.

I finished filtering my water, then stood up and put my pack on.

"Where you headed?"

"Wildcat."

All three of them laughed as though I'd said Mars.

"Honey, you ain't gonna make it there tonight!" one of them said. "You still have to go over Hight and Carter Dome. You'll be lucky if you make it to the hut."

"I'm going to Wildcat tonight."

They were still laughing as I marched away.

Darkness encompassed me as I summited Carter Dome, but as I descended the blocky, stair-like trail into the inky abyss, I could see specks of light emanating from the hut over 1,000 feet below. Slowly they drew closer, until the trail finally leveled out and I passed the inviting glow of the Carter Notch hut.

"Only one more mile," I told myself as I circled a moonlit pond. *And 1,200 vertical feet.*

I plodded up the side of Wildcat Mountain, desperate to sleep. Desperate to be off of my feet. Desperate to prove those pompous old men wrong. I glimpsed the stars holding court above the trees via the narrow strip of sky visible from the trail. Beneath my feet, the incline smoothed out and I felt the faint directional shift of the cool night air. I checked my phone to verify what I could already sense. I'd reached the forested summit of Wildcat Mountain.

~

The next morning I stood inside the bathroom at the Pinkham Notch Visitor Center, wringing as much muddy water out of my socks as I could. Pink hand soap sudsed black liquid free from the fibers of my socks, and my repeated squeezing and rinsing sent it spiraling down the porcelain drain. Several women came in and out of the restroom while I washed my socks (as well as my hands, face, feet, and bandanna) in the sink. Some stares were furtive—others blatant. I made sure to say a cheery hello to every one of them. The responses were as mixed as the stares.

I finished washing out the compression socks I'd brought to sleep in—I'd been wearing them nonstop since my original pair of hiking socks had disintegrated the day after I left the Hiker Hut. I hoped that now they would be clean enough to resume wearing at bedtime. I wiped down the sink and the floor thoroughly, erasing any evidence of my impromptu cleanup, and slipped my bare feet into my dirty shoes. Outside the bathroom, in the lounge area, I unplugged my phone from the wall and climbed the stairs to the store.

I caught the eye of the young woman working behind the counter of the crowded gift shop. "Hi, I'm here to pick up two packages. Heather Anderson."

"I'll be right back," she said.

Standing in an enclosed room with so many freshly showered people, I became keenly aware of my dirt and stench. A couple of minutes later the woman came back with my resupply box in her hands.

"Sign here," she said, sliding the log book toward me and pointing at my name.

"Uh, there's also supposed to be a padded envelope."

"Only one box here for you."

"Would it be possible for you to check again?"

Her sigh was an answer in and of itself. But nonetheless she disappeared into the back again. I could feel my stomach clenching. That envelope held the batteries for my headlamp, annotated maps, and the Awol guidebook pages for the next leg, all the way to my next resupply box at Mountain Meadows Lodge, over 160 miles away. The woman returned and shook her head.

"Nothing back there." She must have sensed my desperation because she added, "Do you have a tracking number?"

"Yes."

I pulled out the spreadsheet from my pocket where I'd recorded my tracking numbers.

"Can you look it up?" I asked.

"No, sorry, but you can use our Wi-Fi."

I pulled out my phone and tried to connect. After several frustrating minutes I realized it wasn't going to load. My package was gone and I was going to have to move onward without it. I turned to the sales area and found some batteries and a second headlamp to replace my failed one. It weighed significantly more, but I needed the additional light. I'd be hiking more hours in the dark as I made my way south, and I didn't want to risk having no light whatsoever if my other headlamp failed. At the counter, I purchased the waterproof light and the batteries and went outside to repack.

My feet basked in the pleasure of clean, dry socks and shoes. Despite the mishap with my maps and batteries, I felt positive now that my feet were free of the Maine mud pits. I quickly ate the town treats from my box and put the new supplies in my food bag. Already puffy clouds were percolating: I needed to get up and over Mount Washington as quickly as possible.

A half mile south of Pinkham Notch I spotted my friend Cheddar, in the midst of his second AT thru-hike, coming toward me.

"Cheddar!" I yelled and ran to give him a hug. He and his hiking companions, Descent and Wander, greeted me as well. I'd known I'd see him at some point, but I was surprised it was so soon.

"How is your hike going?" I asked him.

"It's been really great. How about you? When did you start?"

"August 1. Maine was really hard. So much mud and rain. But, other than my feet, I feel good. How were the Presidentials?"

"It's pretty good up there," he said. "We had clear weather, but there's supposed to be a storm coming in tonight."

"I better get going then. I wish Pinkham hadn't lost my maps."

"What do you mean?"

"They didn't have my package with my maps and Awol pages in it. I have Guthook, but no other resources."

"I think I have mine," Wander said, pawing through her pockets. "For the Presi's at least."

"I have some Awol pages too," Descent said, pulling out some wadded-up pages. "Sorry, they were in my trash."

"Mine are NoBo oriented, but you can probably just reverse it," Wander added, handing over hers.

I quickly assembled enough pages to get me to Kinsman Notch, most of the way through the White Mountains.

"Thank you so much! I really, really appreciate it!"

"No problem.... Now get going!" they cried in unison.

I headed off up the trail as Cheddar, Descent, and Wander continued toward Pinkham Notch and ice cream. I wished I was going with them.

It was only thirteen miles from Pinkham to Mount Washington—the high point of the White Mountains—but I would gain over 4,000 feet ascending and descending near the summits of Mounts Madison, Adams, Jefferson, and Clay along the way. Since most of them were above 4,000 feet, much of my day would be above tree line.

With record-setting wind speeds of over 200 miles per hour, Mount Washington is known for having some of the worst weather in the world. As I dragged myself up the trail, I could see thunderheads building as they grew closer to me. At the top—befuddled by hordes of people—I ducked inside the restaurant. Mount Washington was fierce, but it certainly wasn't a wilderness summit. Overwhelmed by the noise and options of the cafeteria and the dizzying number of people, most of whom had driven or taken the cog train, I simply bought a twenty-ounce coffee and took off.

I gulped the hot beverage as I skipped down the steep talus towards Lakes of the Clouds Hut. "You can take the girl out of Seattle . . ." I laughed to myself, not spilling a drop.

I finally reentered trees and noted the time: 8 p.m. The terrain had slowed me down. I'd done about thirty-seven miles and I needed to hike at least eight more—thirteen would be preferable. The gain and loss, the steep grade, and the talus were holding me firmly at a speed of two miles per hour.

I paused on the ledges as I made my way down the Webster Cliffs, gazing into the almost tangible darkness beyond their precipices—blackness so thick it seemed as solid as the rock under my feet and hands. Once upon a time I'd made a vow to myself here: to thru-hike the Pacific Crest Trail. It seemed like a promise made in another lifetime, by another person altogether.

Since the Chairbacks, I'd vacillated between the desire to give up and the tenacious hope that things would get better. Over and over, I tried to recall what the first weeks of the PCT had been like. There were vague memories of heat, thirst, and pain. Nothing like the wet, cold, rocky miles of the northern AT. One thing I recalled was that although my body eventually hardened to the miles, my mind never did. Every day I had clung desperately to the hope that it would get easier. But no matter how strong my body was, staying focused and intent on the goal was always mentally draining. When I'd finally learned to accept that it wouldn't get easier, I'd been able to let go of that hope without falling apart. But I had to always remind myself that everything that happened along the way was out of my control, that I could only change my reactions, and dedicate myself to putting one foot in front of the other, even when I wanted to stop.

Now that I'd finally cracked forty miles for the day, I was cognizant of my physical self breaking down. My feet ached from the pounding and the raw blisters. Weariness permeated my every cell. I wondered if the decision to focus my training on climbing mountains instead of racking up high-mileage days had been a mistake. Yet, I also knew running twenty miles on well-graded trails wouldn't have prepared me for the hands-on descent I was now doing in the dark.

Raindrops pelted me as the trail evened out into smoother tread. I willed myself forward at a pace approaching three miles per hour, jelly-legged from my day ascending and descending the rocks of the Wildcats and Presidentials.

I wish I'd bought some more food at Pinkham.

I could tell my body craved more fuel. It was adapting to the rigors of the AT faster than it had to those of the PCT. Every day I was easily eating all 2,500 calories of my daily allotment. It wasn't until my next box that my rations would increase: up to 3,000 calories per day. Thankfully, I had the food co-op in Hanover to look forward to before then. My body was adapting, but the hole of sleep deprivation and emotional tug-of-war was not going to stop. It would—I was certain—become worse up until I reached the end of the journey.

~

The early morning miles to Zealand Falls Hut were easy, albeit uncomfortable in the pouring rain. I walked in as the staff— colloquially referred to at every hut as the croo—were serving breakfast.

"Can I fill my water bottle and buy three of those energy bars?" I asked the man who came over to me.

After exchanging twelve dollars for an extra four hundred calories per day, I headed back into the rain. I'd thought it was raining hard before I reached the hut, but as I ascended Zealand Ridge, climbing into a wall of slate-colored water, visibility diminished to less than ten feet.

"Hi!"

I squealed in surprise at the voice, since the man in a red rain jacket had appeared out of the fog at the exact same time he'd spoken. His companion was not far behind.

"Uhm, hi," I said.

"Are you thru-hiking?"

"Yes."

"Want some extra food? We're bailing."

"Uh, sure, yes. Although," I said before pausing, feeling awkward. I still wasn't sure how to define my dietary needs without sounding pretentious. "I have an allergy. To wheat."

"Aw, I got plenty you can have I think," said Red Jacket, seemingly unfazed by this information, or the rain. He set his massive pack on the ground and opened it.

His companion mumbled something about crackers through blue lips and pulled two bars from his pocket. I took them gratefully.

"I'm gonna keep going," he said.

"Ok, yeah, here. Pad Thai!" Red Jacket triumphantly pulled the packaged meal out and handed it to me.

"Thank you!" I tucked it into my own pack. I didn't have the heart to tell him that, without a stove, I wouldn't be able to rehydrate it. It was one of my favorite meals. I'd figure out a way to eat it.

"And anything here," he said, dumping his snack bag out onto the lid of his backpack. "Guess you can't have these." He picked up the mini packs of cookies that had tumbled to the ground.

"Really? Any of this?"

"Yeah, I don't want to carry this shit anymore," he laughed. "In two hours, I'm going to be eating a cheeseburger and fries."

I swooped in and grabbed six more bars as well as a mini bag of chips.

"Thanks so much!"

"Thank you! Enjoy your hike. It's wet up there!" He laughed again—a resounding, deep belly laugh—as he threw everything back into his pack.

I dashed up the trail, ripping into the chips with icy fingers. I devoured two of the energy bars as well, suddenly wishing I'd kept my money at Zealand Hut.

I reached Galehead Hut hours later. The temperature was barely in the forties and the windchill along the exposed ridge-lines had dropped to dangerous levels. I was soaked through my jacket and poncho and the precipitation showed no signs of stopping. The empty dining room building I ducked into wasn't much warmer, but the lack of wind and rain made a huge difference. In the front, past the rows of long tables and benches, the croo had a donation basket set beside a coffee pot, basket of tea bags, and hot water urn. I threw a dollar in the basket and filled a cup of coffee before yanking the pad Thai from my pack and adding hot water.

I sank onto a bench and tried to guide the shaking cup of coffee to my lips, eventually getting enough into my body to slow the shivering. I checked my watch. It had been eight minutes. I refilled my coffee a second time . . . and a third. *Eleven minutes.* The pad Thai wouldn't be fully hydrated, but I didn't want to wait anymore. I began wolfing down the half-crunchy meal.

"Are you thru-hiking?" a man asked, as two preteen boys beside him stared wide-eyed at me.

I hadn't even noticed them come in. They looked wet and I figured they'd just returned from a hike up to Galehead Mountain.

"Yes, I am."

The boys whispered something to their dad.

"Why don't you ask her?" he said.

"Are you going south or north?" the older boy asked.

"South."

"When did you start?"

"August 1."

"That's over forty miles a day!" the father couldn't help but interject.

I smiled and wiped pad Thai off my face with the back of my hand. Then I tipped the package up and drank the rest of the liquid.

"She's cooler than Bear Grylls!" the youngest one exclaimed. His stage whisper to his father was met with a roar of laughter.

"I think that's the best compliment I've ever gotten," I said, smiling at him.

I threw my trash away and took a deep breath. It was easier to step outside into the furor of the storm with their admiring eyes on me.

The warmth of the food and coffee in my belly lasted only a few miles. The trail along Franconia Ridge was exposed and, despite moving as fast as possible, I could not stay warm. The rain finally began to taper as I dropped below 4,000 feet near the Liberty Springs campsite. Even so, it seemed as though I would never thaw.

I lost elevation rapidly as the dirt trail caked my new shoes and socks in mud. My goal for camp was Eliza Brook shelter, eleven miles beyond the Kinsman Peaks. At the bottom of the descent I'd merge with easy trail and bike paths, which, combined with thinning clouds and lack of wind, would result in faster miles—I hoped.

I might be able to crack forty miles today after all.

It was a rueful observation. I knew the Kinsmans might crush me, but I was so far behind schedule I had to try to get past the two rocky, exposed summits that day. Suddenly my feet slid out from under me and I landed in the mud, banging my knee on a rock.

"I'm so sick of mud!" I couldn't help but scream.

I sat for a moment. *Just get to Hanover. Things will get better in Vermont. Just get through New Hampshire.*

I got to my feet. I had told myself a hundred times to just make it past Hanover to the smoother trail of Vermont. Some days I felt like I could do it. Other days I didn't. Some days I told myself I could quit at the New Hampshire border in Hanover. Other days I told myself I couldn't quit until I finished Vermont—150 miles farther. Most nights I felt an extreme hopelessness brought on by the bone-deep fatigue of the day as I crawled into my sleeping bag, physically destroyed and always short of my goal. Each morning it would lessen somewhat. But every setback along the way eroded my dream that what I was attempting was possible.

"TRAIL DETOUR."

The bold words on the sign snapped me out of my self-pitying spiral. I stooped to read the notice and study the diagram.

"CASCADE BROOK BRIDGE is gone. Brook is IMPASSABLE during high water."

I said the words slowly out loud to let them sink in. The diagram showed a route on bike paths and trails that crossed the brook elsewhere. Pulling out my phone, I tried to figure out the reroute, but it wasn't in the app. I suddenly felt the limitations of not having my guidebook pages. I felt panic as well. The simplified hand-drawn map was not clear enough to navigate from and the detour looked many miles longer. I shook my head to clear it and surged forward, following the white blazes. *I have to do this hike perfectly.*

"It can't be that bad," I reassured myself. "None of the comments in Guthook mention taking it."

I heard the roar of Cascade Brook a full quarter mile before I reached it. Although I'd finally warmed up, I felt ice churn in my stomach when I saw it. Cascade Brook did indeed look impassable. It reminded me of the rivers in the High Sierra during peak melt—rivers that could easily throw you down, pin you beneath a rock, and crush the air from your lungs. I stood on the bank and took several deep breaths as I studied the wide, cavorting flow. *Boulders at the trail crossing. Small waterfall downstream. Wider, flatter water upstream. Two channels.* These observations filed, I waded in to test the current and was almost immediately knocked off my feet. I stabbed frantically with my trekking poles as my shoes slipped on the slimy rocks. I managed to stabilize myself and retreat to the bank.

"Holy shit!"

I moved upstream and read the river from there. The giant submerged rocks made holes and hydraulic keepers that terrified me. But as long as I could keep my feet down it might be possible to cross a hundred yards up. Much more tentatively, I made my way into the water. I worked my way across slowly while angling upstream, where the river appeared more passable. The farther I went, the more obstacles I saw. Weaving around boulders and holes in crotch-deep water, I once again felt the warmth of my body ebbing away. I finally reached a bend where it looked possible to finish crossing and began to make my way toward the trees splitting the channels. I felt the river pull harder and harder until my poles—planted in the strongest part of the current—vibrated with the power of the water. I could barely keep myself upright. My eyes tracked to where whitewater frothed as it flung itself over rocks and off of the drop. I knew there was a serious waterfall a short distance downstream. My mind raced to the recent death of an acquaintance while fording a river in the Brooks Range.

I can't.

I stood frozen, uncertain if I could even lift one pole without compromising my balance. Panic ran through me at the speed of the water I was immersed in. I closed my eyes and breathed calmly, dispersing the fear into the water and away from me. Slowly, I reversed my progress. I couldn't move any faster in retreat than I had in my cautious approach without falling in. My body shook violently with chills, and I was barely able to feel my feet and legs, which slowed me even more.

I resisted the call of the river, just as I had in the throes of the Little Sandy on Mount Hood: *"Come with me."*

I stumbled out of the water on wobbly legs like a sailor suddenly turned landlubber. My numb limbs collapsed and I landed on the muddy embankment, crawling a few feet away from the water to compose myself. I knelt there on hands and knees, convulsing with shivers, adrenaline, and relief. As pins and needles stabbed my legs, signaling the return of blood flow, I started to cry—not because of the pain, but because of the loss. This setback was the final blow to my ambition.

"I'm done," I said, rocking back and forth. "I'm done."

After a couple of minutes, I was finally able to stand. I looked at my watch and was shocked to see I'd been in the river for half an hour. I looked north on the AT—white blazes beckoned me backward to the last road crossing in Franconia Notch and the warm hostels of nearby North Woodstock. I could go there and call Apple Pie. She would take me to the airport. I could go to my parents. I could accept my complete failure once and for all. I could live with the fluke of the PCT. It no longer permeated my dreams or my daily life now that I no longer spoke of it. Only on trail did the specter of Anish the Ghost haunt me. *I tried. Now I can let it go forever.*

My body shuddered again. I realized—now that the adrenaline was wearing off—I faced a real risk of developing hypothermia. For fourteen hours I'd been pushing myself through extreme conditions, just barely staying warm enough, and then I'd stood in a frigid river for thirty minutes. Dizzy, I realized I couldn't remember the last time I'd eaten.

In the morning. I will quit in the morning.

I needed one last night in the tent where I could grieve in peace. By rote I established camp on the muddy ground near the river that had asked for my life. I gave it one last look before zipping shut the vestibule. It *had* taken my life. It had taken the last hope I'd had that I was *something*. It had answered me definitively: I was not.

I crawled into my bag, throwing my wet clothes into the corner, not caring if they dried. *Who cares? I'm quitting in the morning.* I ate my dinner and as many snacks as I wanted until—for the first time in days—I was sated. Snuggling deeper into my sleeping bag, I curled around a chocolate bar and waited for my scant body heat to warm me and my dessert. Through the slim gap under my vestibule I watched squirrels bounce around the woodland floor. A blaze ten yards away called to mind my New Year's dream.

"I thought it meant success out here. Answers," I mumbled to myself and the squirrels. "I guess I did get answers. Just not the ones I wanted."

I rolled onto my back and listened to the river. It sang songs I couldn't understand—no longer calling me. Mentally and physically exhausted, I ate the chocolate slowly, letting it melt and coat my mouth. I began composing the list of things I'd need to do when I reached town. Soon the list became too long to hold in my tired brain, so I pulled out the plastic bag where I stored my spreadsheets. I stared at the optimistic schedule and shook my head. *All those forty-five-to-fifty-mile days.* I recalled the sunny days on the PCT. I'd never been covered in mud, scrambling hand over hand on wet rocks out there. The AT had always been more difficult. *Too difficult for me to set a record on.*

I wrote down a short list of people to call and a to-do list. Then I jotted down the day's thirty miles at the bottom of the string of mileages. *Eighteen miles short for today. This is it. Too many setbacks. I can't come back from this. I'm not strong enough.*

"I did my best. It just wasn't good enough," I told the squirrels outside my tent.

I lay down and turned the alarm off on my watch. There would be no need to wake up at four in the morning. I pulled my hat over my eyes and put my earplugs in. I pondered the words Jennifer Pharr Davis had written in her book *Called Again* about her record-setting hike. She'd focused on doing her best every day, rather than on the goal, since there was nothing more anyone could do than their best.

Each day I'd done my best and yet each day I'd come up short of my goal. Every night I went to bed demoralized and every morning I felt the pressure to achieve. I'd been riding this vicious cycle over rocks, through mud, and in and out of torrential precipitation. Here, on the bank of Cascade Brook, I'd finally been derailed. Failure was harsh and it would be tough to move past, but I was relieved to know I'd no longer swirl in the endless loop of unanswered questions.

~

Sunshine woke me up—not with its brightness, but with the warmth of the greenhouse effect building inside my tent. Similar to the morning at the Kennebec, I sat up, initially confused by the obvious lateness of the morning and pulled my earplugs out. The sound of Cascade Brook made my stomach clench in dismay, reminding me of everything that had happened the day before. It was 6:30 a.m. *I slept twelve hours.*

I ate, pulled my wet clothes on, and packed slowly, shivering in the soggy garments. *There's no rush today,* I told myself. At seven I stepped out into the sunlight and took down my tent. Slinging my pack on, I walked over to the river, feeling like I should thank it for allowing me to live—and for providing me with answers, even though they weren't the ones I'd wanted.

I was surprised to see that the water level had fallen by several feet. The brook was still high and flowing fast, but it was no longer the frothing tumult it had been half a day earlier. Like a moth drawn to candlelight, I stepped in. I sucked in a great gulp of air, shocked by the still icy water. Prodding with my poles, I moved carefully—always ensuring a solid foothold before I moved an inch. A few minutes later I was across the river. I turned to look back at my former campsite in confusion and shock. I'd had no intention of crossing, yet here I was.

"You're stronger than you think."

I heard the words Cascade Brook called in farewell as I turned southward and headed down the trail. *Maybe my FKT attempt isn't over after all?*

The river had not taken anything. Instead it had given me something great: hope.

~

I covered the mile and a half to Lonesome Lake Hut in thirty minutes. Setting my pack down on the porch, I dug inside and pulled out the baggie containing my schedule and list of resupplies and tracking numbers. I carefully tore the page in half and put the resupply list back into its waterproof home. Then I scanned the column of typed goal mileage numbers and handwritten actual ones lined up like a protracted math problem. After so many delays, the typed schedule was now simply unattainable.

All I can do is my best. Every day. One step, one blaze at a time. Until Springer. And my best will get me there, no matter how long it takes.

Crumpling it in my hand, I threw the schedule into the trash can with my wrappers from the dinner binge the night before. My best had been reframed as I stood dripping on the south side of Cascade Brook, astonished to even be standing there.

My best was not dependent on meeting numbers typed on a piece of paper. My best was finding my limit every day, refusing to relent until I could no longer go on. My best would have to be committed to over and over again, no matter the hardships or setbacks I faced. My best would be what it was and I would once again have to accept what was and what was not. Filling my water from the pitchers inside, I headed out toward North and South Kinsman.

The rain came again as I climbed above 4,000 feet past North Kinsman. I traversed to South Kinsman and began to clamber down the class three descent. For the first time in the entire hike I was more aware of the rocks beneath me than how far I had to go. As water sluiced past me, my grip slipped on the precarious purchase. I threw my trekking poles down the waterslide and swung to face the rocks. After down climbing the slippery facade I reclaimed my poles. Blood trickled down my scraped legs as I strode onward, my sodden dress clinging to them. I still had to climb Moosilauke—then I'd be free of the White Mountains.

Hours later I spotted the orange sign marking the summit of Mount Moosilauke through the vapor-laden air. Laughing, I reached out and grabbed it. *I made it through the Whites!* After slipping a poncho on to keep the rain lashing me at bay, I snapped a picture of myself. Then I leaned into the wind and pushed on toward the tree line on the south side. Once I reached it I knew—despite the blocky summits of Mount Cube and Smarts Mountain between me and Hanover—I was essentially done with the technical trail of Maine and New Hampshire. I was almost to Vermont. After nearly two weeks of relentless eighteen-hour days bashing my feet and body against seemingly endless rocks, mud, and roots, the hardest terrain was now firmly behind me. So, I hoped, was the roller coaster of emotions I'd ridden while pushing myself to my absolute limit through Maine and New Hampshire. Now, I would simply do my best and set the fastest pace that I could to Georgia. I tucked my hands into my waistband, seeking the smidge of warmth seeping through the poncho.

The clouds above me thinned as I hammered down the mountain. As the day warmed, I began to thaw. Slowly, the rocks grew sparser and then—as suddenly as daybreak—I was in verdant forest on a ribbon of soft, dirt trail. The land was dry and the wall of rocks I'd been fighting was now behind me. So were the exposed mountaintops I'd crossed despite lightning, hail, and rain falling so thickly I could only see a few feet. In the days behind me, I'd cried thinking my hike was over too many times to count. Yet always the magic of the mountains—whether crane, porcupine, moose, or river—had reassured me that all was not lost. And now, having released myself from my schedule, I was moving forward faster than ever. I had to let go of my own expectations in order to find out what I was truly capable of doing. Despite the hardships, I felt afire with hope. Anish was finally ready to embrace the Appalachian Trail in all her rocky, wild, forested glory.

"Welcome back," she said.

"Thank you," I whispered. "Thank you."

~

Even with the late start and the difficulty of the Kinsmans and Moosilauke, I'd still covered thirty-three miles in twelve hours, four hours faster than my typical sixteen. I fell asleep to coyote song, and at four in the morning I'd flown into the dusky light— an owl intent on finding her roost—in the upstairs break room of the co-op.

Striding into the busy store midday, I was overwhelmed by color, sound, and choice. Suddenly my world of mud brown, gray rock, and green leaf was lost in the chaos of commodity. I wandered the aisles, putting everything that looked enticing into my handbasket. I chose item after item from the deli. When I could hold nothing more, I lined up at the register to pay for my forage.

"Are you hiking the AT?" the clerk asked, smiling.

"Yes. Southbound."

The woman pointed toward the stairs, confirming what the guidebook had said. "You can use our employee break room to eat and charge your phone."

It was quiet upstairs, and I settled into a corner of the room with my devices plugged in and my resupply items and food from the deli arrayed on the table in front of me. I felt right at home. It was identical to the co-op I'd been working at in Washington.

Sipping a large coffee, I dove into the baked tofu while also removing excess packaging from gluten-free cookies and crackers and adding them to my food bag. Finished with the tofu, I started on the Greek salad, stuffing the trash from the last stretch into the empty cracker box. Next was the gelato—I finished that with the last of my coffee.

Having organized my resupply and packed away several thousand calories into my stomach, I settled back into the seat. There weren't any artificial lights on in the room; everything was lit by pearly sunlight filtering through the high windows, like the woods at twilight. I rested my hands on my contented belly and sighed.

Even though it was distended from the feast, I could still feel the toll the long miles for days on end had taken under my fingers. *I've lost a lot of weight already. Just as I did in the first two weeks of the PCT.* My poor feet were far more blistered and chafed than they had ever been. I feared infection, but since they were bathed in a constant state of wetness and mud, I could do little except smear some antibiotic cream on them each night before bed, and hope it would be enough.

Beyond the obvious injuries, there was also the memory of an unknown trauma lurking inside me. I still had no idea what had caused me to pee blood for twenty-four hours. My urine had been clear for many days now, but the memory of the Merlot color haunted the corners of my mind. *Had I lost function in a kidney? Was it merely bladder chafe? Or rhabdomyolysis? A UTI that cleared up on its own? A small kidney stone? Or something else I could not guess?*

After a few minutes I resumed packing, adding up the calories as I went to ensure I was leaving town with my requisite 3,000 per day. Happily, I discovered I'd overbought. Tearing open a bag of chips, I munched while looking at the upcoming trail in Guthook.

"I really need to get going," I told myself.

I'd been in the store for two hours, but now I was out of things to do and full of fuel to hike. My phone was at 97 percent. Yet the comfort of sitting still anchored me to the chair. Despite my resolve to do my best and continue the hike, the thought of moving didn't appeal to me at all. *Didn't I say I could quit here?*

I coached myself through the conflicting emotions and desires. "You can quit after Vermont," I said out loud. "If you're still spinning your wheels and desperate, you can quit then. But give it a state with fewer rocks. Hike on an actual trail for a while." I pried myself out of the seat and headed down the stairs.

While crossing the bridge over the Connecticut River, I stopped midway where "VT/NH" was etched into the cement. I closed my eyes and my spirit reached for the river. I could discern it there—coursing below my feet—singing the same farewell song as Cascade Brook.

You're stronger than you believe. Just do your best.

I stepped across the artificial line humans arrogantly believed could cleave a river and entered Vermont. It felt marvelous to let go.

FATIGUE

IT WAS ONLY FORTY-TWO miles from Hanover to my next box. I relished the variety of food I'd purchased, but despite the influx of calories and relatively easy tread, I started flagging shortly after nightfall. I gave in and slept a mere eight miles past the border. In the morning, my alarm was met with groggy floundering before I stumbled through the quiet forest, then a still-sleeping village, and up and across expansive fields.

As my grogginess faded, the day became repetitive: ascend through a field, wind through maple trees, descend through a field, cross a road, repeat. After several iterations the sky blackened. I scrambled up the trail as it followed a ladder set against a rock face and scurried through the trees.

"At least Vermont gives you ladders," I muttered.

I was moving no faster than before. My legs still felt like lead. My head wasn't any lighter and my mind was torpid. Wanting only to sleep, I sank onto a perfect sitting rock and hunched over.

"I thought I'd feel better by now. It's easier. I have more food. Why don't I feel better?"

Even a single day of food on my back seemed to weigh more than I could bear. I'd let go of expectations, but it hadn't brought a magical release from the weariness.

"It's like riding a bicycle . . . but my feet hurt more."

I laughed at my own joke. It was true. My body clearly remembered what an FKT entailed, even if I'd forgotten. The fatigue was deep and overwhelming . . . and it wasn't going to get any better.

Hours later, at the Mountain Meadows Resort, I got my box and rapidly switched things out. The staff were not welcoming and I wanted to be on my way as soon as I could. Repacked, I donned rain gear and headed out into the sprinkles, toward where Vermont's two-hundred-plus-mile Long Trail intersected with the Appalachian Trail.

Dusk came early, the last hour of sunlight blocked by a storm. I hiked up the steep climb to the Maine Junction where I would cross the Long Trail. Reaching the spot at eight o'clock, I shone my headlamp at every sign in turn, confused. Both the AT and the Long Trail were blazed in white, so I took the time to be certain I knew which was the correct trail before beginning the equally steep descent. I would encounter the Long Trail again near the top of Killington Peak and follow it south while it ran concurrent with the AT.

Though acute climbs and equally sharp downhills that take you the hardest route between points A and B are a continuous theme along the AT, I had no patience for it at that moment.

"Stupid trail," I muttered. "I'm *so* tired." I crossed Route 4 and headed toward Killington.

"C'mon, Anish," I cheered myself on. "It's only six miles to the top." *And 2,000 vertical feet.*

Initially the trail was mellow, but it grew steadily steeper as I went. My pace became a ponderous grind. Mist turned to drizzle. Time halted. My brain wandered into the blackness, leaving my eyes to focus on the leaf-littered trail illuminated by two beams of light. I was utterly and completely spent.

"I've got to be getting close," I told myself when my watched chimed ten.

Pulling out my phone, I opened the Guthook app and waited impatiently for it to assess my location. Although I wished it would go faster, I was also thankful for the excuse to stand still. When the blue dot finally appeared on the screen, I shook the phone in disbelief. I had only gone a mile and a half.

I closed my phone. I was desperately tired. More than that, I was thoroughly fed up with my body.

"You're worthless!" I hissed to myself.

As though the sky wanted to reprimand me for chastising my body for its incompetence, it began to rain in earnest. I trudged onward at a snail's pace for another hour. Then, soaked and forlorn, I went off trail, kicked a few branches off of the soggy leaves, and began setting up my tent. *This will work.*

In the light of my twin headlamps I saw bright red specks scurrying into the darkness. I squatted down, curious, and waited patiently for my weary brain to decipher what was there: dozens of red-orange salamanders. I peeled up the edges of my tent and cleared the area of amphibians before I crawled in. I was too worn out to eat, a poor decision, but I ignored my better judgment and slipped into unconsciousness thankfully.

~

I reached Cooper Lodge near the summit of Killington at six the next morning. If anyone had spent the night there, they were gone by the time I arrived. The sparse forest offered little protection from the heavy rain. Despite sleeping, I felt as exhausted after ninety minutes of hiking as I had the night before. I'd forgotten what crushing fatigue felt like. It was easy to remember the sunny, cruising miles of the PCT in Northern California, where I felt invincible. It was much more difficult to remember the complete and utter lassitude of the desert.

I looked around, unwittingly searching for a place to camp. Realizing what I was doing, I forced myself to hike past the shelter and up the last rise. I could barely lift my feet high enough to clear obstacles on the ground. Every molecule of my body seemed to have reached the specific gravity of gold.

Unable to take another step, I sank down onto the muddy ground and leaned back on my pack. My head rolled backward, tilting my face skyward. I couldn't even muster the strength to move it away from the splattering drops. Vaguely, I remembered my dad telling me that turkeys are so stupid they look up at the rain, drowning themselves in heavy downpours. *Maybe they aren't dumb, just tired.*

Rain pelted my frigid skin, forming rivulets that trickled down my neck and under the collar of my rain jacket. I was unaware of anything except their icy tracks snaking down my arms, meandering along my palms, and finally dripping off the tips of my fingers.

"How did I ever do this? I'm so damn *tired!*"

How did *I do it?* I rolled the question around in my overtired brain, letting it wash down my cheeks with the tears that had joined the raindrops. *How did I set an FKT?*

There were no answers in the gray sky or the hushed sound of a dripping forest. I dug my heels into the black mud and thought about my first thru-hike.

How did I hike this trail when I was twenty-one, with no idea what I was doing?

I'd been fresh out of college with five hundred dollars to my name. The AT was my second multi-night backpacking trip—the first one an utter disaster which I'd cut short.

"What happened to me? What's happened to Anish?"

Choking on the rain now, I rolled to my side. I didn't want to keep hiking, but I also didn't want to die a turkey's death on the slopes of Killington Peak. Covered in mud and soaked to the bone, I'd begun to shiver.

"You shivered dusk to dawn those first three weeks," I told myself.

I remembered that clearly enough—how I'd started the AT with no sleeping bag, no rain jacket, no tent, and no bug spray. Each evening, I'd wrap myself in a space blanket and shiver until daybreak. Then I'd put my wet clothes back on and hike nonstop until evening, just to stay warm. I finally made enough money to buy a clearance sleeping bag by working an odd job in Hot Springs, North Carolina. I never did acquire a rain jacket for that trip.

I looked down at my poncho, rain jacket, and muddy shoes. As bad as my feet were, they were better than they had been when I'd started my hike in 2003. Then, I'd hiked over half the trail in a couple pairs of five dollar shoes I'd bought at the dollar store.

"I started with ten toenails and finished with one," I remembered. In spite of everything, I managed a small laugh.

Here I was in high-tech gear, comfortable footwear, and over a decade of experience under my hip belt, and yet I was lying in the mud and rain, bawling.

"I can't do this."

Can't or won't? My ruminations began pulling up memories faster. Not from the PCT FKT . . . which seemed oddly unrelated. Instead my mind was bringing forward all of the hardships I'd faced on this very ribbon of mud and rocks when I was a neophyte backpacker. *Anish, you survived on Pop-Tarts and peanut butter. By Pennsylvania you were so malnourished your hair was falling out in clumps. Remember what you did?*

"I braided it and walked on," I said aloud.

Remember what happened after that? A tooth broke off. What did you do?

"I spit it out and kept walking."

Why?

"Because nothing was going to stop me."

Do you remember ever having a bad day on that hike?

"No."

Why not?

"I was hiking with determination and passion for adventure."

I sat up and watched the water flowing down the center of the trail, each drop finding its own path to follow through the cycle back to reincarnation as rain yet again. "I'm sitting here literally talking to myself in the rain."

Slowly, a realization worked its way through the lethargy filling my skull. *Pain and hardship are integral to any thru-hike, as they are to life in general. It is suffering that is a mindset.*

What would my younger self have said if she saw me sitting here crying simply because I was tired? I smiled—I knew exactly what that girl would have said: *Suck it up, buttercup.*

"Suck it up, buttercup," I whispered to myself.

Then I laughed. It felt empowering to laugh just as everything seemed to be collapsing in on me. I'd decided in that moment—even if it was going to take a thousand conscious choices every day—that I would choose not to suffer. There would be no drudgery on my hike. I would move forward with passion for adventure. Just as I always had.

I heaved myself up, soaked to the bone and muddy, grimacing as the pooled rainwater rolled down my body and into my shoes. I laughed again, this time at the complete ridiculousness of the past fifteen minutes.

"Suck it up, buttercup," I said again, louder, and stepped forward.

Moving at almost three miles per hour, I walked until nearly midnight and arose the next morning at the first hint of light. Throughout Vermont's respite from rocks, I repeated this cycle again and again. The trail would tell me the answers when the time was right. I just needed to keep hiking until then.

11

NIGHT HIKING

SOUTH OF KILLINGTON THE weather grew hot and more humid. Gnats and flies joined the omnipresent swarms of mosquitoes that chewed on me mercilessly. I sprayed on bug repellent only to feel it glide down my sweat-slicked skin and into my clothing. Now in Massachusetts, I passed the rocky area near Pete's Spring and picked up the pace. I was almost to Route 2—important because of the Stop & Shop supermarket just a short distance off the trail. I hadn't noticed much of anything over the last few miles—except for leaving Vermont—because I was busy thinking about all the food I was going to buy when I got there. At the road, I turned right, but after half a mile I still hadn't seen the supermarket. I pulled out my phone.

To my dismay, I realized that I'd turned onto Massachusetts Avenue. I had missed the turn that crossed the Hoosic River and led to Route 2. Backtracking as fast as I could, I stormed back onto the white-blazed route—obvious now that I was watching for it. When I finally reached the highway I sped westward, and soon spotted the huge grocery store on the left. I grabbed a cart and walked into the blessed air conditioning.

Immediately inside the front door was the natural foods section. I wandered up each aisle, grabbing every gluten-free indulgence that caught my eye. In line, I stared at my half-full cart. *I can't get all this!* Chagrined, I backed out of the line and retreated to the natural foods corner to add up the calories. I returned a third of the cart to the shelves.

After paying, I found a bench near an outlet outside and sat down to consume my pile of delicious treats. I plugged my phone in, opened a can of chili, and began wolfing it down, alternating with spoonfuls of avocado. Unable to resist, I sampled some of everything I'd bought to eat while hiking. I polished off the meal with a banana and a pint of ice cream, savoring every single bite.

My phone was charged and I was beyond sated. It had been a little over an hour since I'd arrived in town, which, combined with the extra mile I hiked when I'd made the wrong turn, meant I needed to get moving. I wanted to get over the summit of Mount Greylock—the high point of Massachusetts—that night. While packing everything up, I discovered I still had a bottle of kombucha to drink.

I hefted it. I wasn't sure there'd be a trash can at the trailhead and I certainly didn't want to carry the glass bottle to the next town. But, I also didn't want it to go to waste. I considered dumping out my water bottle and filling it with kombucha. In the end, I decided to chug it.

Before I even got across the parking lot it was obvious I'd eaten too much. And chugging the kombucha, on top of it all, had clearly been a very bad choice. I lay down in a ditch and tried to breathe. I felt sweaty and chilled at the same time—like I was either going to die or vomit.

"I really don't care which, just get on with it," I moaned.

After a few minutes, things stabilized. I managed to get up and slowly make my way out of town and back to the trail. Light was fading quickly and my queasy stomach threatened to revolt anytime I tried to increase my lethargic pace. There was no way I was going to reach the high point of Massachusetts before bed. By morning my body had assimilated the thousands of calories and I felt energized as I climbed. Greylock was moody, greeting me with leaden skies as I crossed near the summit shortly after sunup. I'd hiked over six hundred miles south, and the amount of time each day that I needed my headlamp was now noticeable. Each morning I walked forty-five minutes by its light; each night, an hour or more. There was also far less rock scrambling, which meant it was easier to follow the white blazes in the dark. The trade-off of light for easier terrain seemed favorable. My body had survived the drubbing and was now covering miles consistently.

"Only three days to new shoes," I encouraged my thrashed feet. The shoes I'd acquired in Pinkham Notch were torn, the tread scoured smooth under the toes. And the lone pair of socks I'd worn since then had a hole the size of a quarter on the ball of each foot. Though the blisters on the soles of my feet had begun to harden into calloused skin, my feet reminded me continually of the hardship in carrying me over forty miles, day after day.

The sun shone brilliantly as I emerged from the forest near Cheshire, Massachusetts, and made my way down from the high country. I was thirsty and out of water as increasing humidity wrapped me in a sultry blanket, yet there was something about the emerald cornfields and trilling songbirds that made my heart soar above the swelter. The white blazes skirted a cornfield and I followed the trail at the end of the rows, overwhelmed by homesickness.

"I miss you," I whispered to my parents.

I missed standing barefoot in the midsummer humidity, digging my toes into the rich earth of our garden. The long, straight rows of vegetables my father tended extending southward— perpendicular to the rows of flowers my mother grew to nurture her beehives. I missed helping her lay thick layers of newspaper with mulch shoveled on top, so we wouldn't have to weed, even though I complained at the time.

We would all work hard when the peas, corn, and tomatoes began coming in by the wheelbarrow load. As much as I'd whined, I now found myself wishing for an evening on the back deck shelling endless peas into five-gallon buckets while fireflies flickered. Or husking dozens of ears of corn until my hands were sticky with pollen and I was covered in silks. Those nights that I sat with both my parents in meditative work were quiet: small talk and stories interspersed with long periods of silence, interrupted only by the plunk of peas into a bucket or the buzz of uncoupling husks. Seeing the fields on the AT made my heart squeeze hard with nostalgia.

"Anish?!"

I stopped, startled out of my memories. A northbound hiker was standing directly in front of me.

"Yes."

"Wow! I'm honored to meet you," he said, shaking my hand. "I'm Pony."

"Um, hi."

"I don't want to keep you. I just wanted you to know what an inspiration you are."

"Well, thank you. Very much."

"Oh, and if you need water or to charge anything you can stop at the church up here in Cheshire. They let the hikers use the hall."

"Thank you."

Pony waved and continued north. I hastened my steps toward the quaint New England town—the church was listed in the Guthook app and I easily found it. All was quiet except for the sound of nearby lawn mowers as I followed posted signs directing hikers into the hush and shadows of the church hall. Surprised to find myself the only hiker there, I plugged my phone into an outlet, thankful for the delicious coolness and peace of the vacant room. I set my pack down by my phone and walked across the hallway to use the restroom.

It felt good to wash my hands and face with soap. I stared at the tanned visage in the mirror. I knew it was mine, but yet it was also unfamiliar. There were now angles below my cheekbones where the subcutaneous fat had melted. The blue eyes were clear, but full of weariness. The skin below them sagged. The face in the mirror looked tired. I pushed my fingers through my short hair in an attempt to bring familiarity to my appearance, briefly remembering when I clipped the dreadlocks from my head in a hotel room. Though I'd grown used to seeing Anish—tanned, trail-thin, and dirty—my reflection still felt unfamiliar in some ways. I smiled at myself. It was the smiling woman in the mirror that I recognized. I turned off the faucet and retraced my steps to the hall.

"Hello."

"Oh, hi!" I started.

For the second time in an hour the presence of another human jarred me out of my reveries.

"Welcome. Are you planning to stay tonight?" the woman asked me.

"No, I just came to get water."

The woman smiled and motioned toward the door into the side yard.

"There's a spigot outside you can use. Feel free to rest inside if you'd like."

"Thank you."

After she left the room I returned to my pack, pulled out my bottles, and went outside. Returning to the oppressive heat and humidity after being in the air-conditioned building nearly knocked me off my feet. I filled my bottles, resisting the urge to dump one over my head. I chugged a liter and looked at my watch. *I really need to get going.*

The unplanned stop had already eaten up forty-five minutes. Massachusetts and Connecticut were easier terrain and I was supposed to be making up for lost time. Instead I was giving in to the temptation to sit in an air-conditioned room. I ran back inside, unplugged my phone, and threw it into my pack before I was tempted to stay any longer. *I'll be in the town of Dalton in nine miles.*

"Great, more temptation," I muttered to myself as I hurried back into the forest.

Three hours later I was traveling down Dalton's Main Street.

"Do not look for ice cream. Do not look for ice cream. Do not look for soda. Do not look for soda."

I made the turn onto Depot Street, leaving the businesses of Main Street behind. Now I simply had to hike along residential streets, cross the railroad tracks, and I'd be back in the woods— and away from temptation for the rest of the day.

"Hey there!"

I looked to my right to see several hikers sitting at a picnic table in the shade, drinking sodas. I waved. *Keep going.* I knew it had to be Tom's yard. He was a trail angel, listed in Guthook's app and Awol's guide, who provided water and sometimes tent camping to AT hikers. *There's a creek up ahead. You don't need to stop.*

"You want a soda?"

I stopped at the edge of the lawn. I very much did want a soda. A *cold* soda.

"Sure."

I walked over to the table and took off my pack.

"I'm Tom," one of the people said. I sat down alongside him, feeling a slight whoosh of resignation pass out of my lungs, but I forgot it as soon as Tom put a chilled Coke into my hands.

"Hi, thank you. I'm Anish."

"Another early southbounder," one of the other hikers observed.

"I guess so."

"I've only seen about ten so far this year," Tom said. "Including this guy." He pointed at the hiker who had spoken.

"Yeah, I'm making good time." I took a huge gulp.

"I haven't seen you before. When did you start?" the southbounder asked.

"The first."

The four men sitting at the table were quiet. I knew they were waiting for the rest of the sentence, just like everyone else who'd asked that question. I hoped they'd simply fill in the month they felt made the most sense, like other people had. I finished my soda.

"The first of what?" the southbounder finally asked.

"The first. Of the month. August."

I was met with blank stares.

"Tom, can I fill my water?"

"Oh, sure. It's over there," he said, pointing at a spigot.

"Thanks so much." I carried my bottles over to it.

"You mean you started three weeks ago?" the southbounder asked.

"Yeah."

"That's insane! Like forty miles a day or something."

"Yeah." I returned to the table and put the water in my backpack.

Tom was grinning at the other hiker's shock.

"Thanks so much, Tom. I really appreciate it."

"You're welcome. Good luck."

"Bye!" I waved and bolted back onto the sidewalk.

The sugar in my bloodstream powered me up Warner Hill. I felt incredibly grateful to be back in the peace of the woods. Aside from brief greetings with a few other hikers, I was free to coil into myself. It wasn't until the quick succession of human interactions that day that I realized how internalized I already was. Thinking back to my disjointed conversations along the Pacific Crest Trail, I remembered how after days of hiking alone I'd seemingly lost the ability to converse with my own species. Yet, I spoke freely with the trees and the wind. No words were needed for that feral telepathy.

I passed by the turnoff for the October Mountain shelter sooner than expected. The temperature had dropped as the sky blackened—yet another storm was coming. *Would the daily torrents ever stop?* I hurried, spurred not only by the desire to escape the storm, but also to make up for the hours lost between yesterday's binge-induced sloth and the many creature comforts of today.

I was on the shore of Finerty Pond when the storm hit me from behind. Thunder reverberated off of the hills. Rain fell in sheets. Wind gusted across the water, shaking the trees behind me like a lion stalking in tall grass. The sound of it grew closer at a rapid speed: there was no way for me to outpace the tempest. I ran along the open trail, relieved to reach the partial shelter of the forest at the end of the lake. The trees danced in the gale and the trail became a river as I pushed up Becket Mountain. My soaked dress clung to my thighs. Puddles formed in my shoes and sloshed over the sides. I could hardly conceive of the arid PCT.

Looking up, I squinted against the raindrops. *It will be dark soon.* I reached the summit, and as I began descending the rain slowed to a drizzle. For the first time in several days I started to shiver. I stopped briefly to throw my rain jacket on and pull out my headlamp. By its light I continued toward the dull roar of the Massachusetts Turnpike in the distance. Beyond that, I'd have to travel another five miles through the Goose Pond Reservation before I could camp; the only legal camping site in the reservation was well off trail.

"It's going to be a late night," I said, bemoaning my inability to pass up creature comforts.

Without a schedule, it was up to me to push myself. On the PCT I'd done everything within my power to reach my predetermined camp spots each day. Now I was so far off schedule it didn't seem to matter. I aimed for forty-five miles every day, but seldom met it.

Am I just hiking now? I wondered to myself. *Or am I still trying to set a record? Because if I'm just hiking, I'm going to sleep more.*

Matt Kirk's self-supported record was fifty-eight days and change. I'd set out at a sub-fifty-day pace. The weather, the Kennebec, the rocks, the mud, and Cascade Brook had irrevocably quashed that itinerary. Now I wasn't sure where I was in relation to any record. If I wasn't going to try to set it then why was I hiking until the witching hour so often? Or waking up at four in the morning for that matter.

I sure do miss sleep.

The sound of the highway was nearly deafening now as the trail paralleled the road. My hair prickled and I felt a primal uneasiness creep along my spine as I followed the trail down under overpass pilings to ascend a ramp and use the pedestrian bridge over the highway. Graffiti covered every inch of concrete illuminated by my headlamp. *The cars are so close.* Their rapid pace and noise was disconcerting, and I was gripped by an overwhelming urge to flee. I ran up and across the overpass and down the other side—my hackles didn't lower until I was almost two miles away. *I know how animals must feel near highways,* I thought. Soon after my fight or flight response ebbed, I reached the sign for the Upper Goose Pond shelter, which was a half mile off trail.

The caretakers serve coffee and breakfast.

Sinking down to rest at the junction, I thought back to when I'd stayed at the Upper Goose Pond shelter in 2003. The heaps of food I'd consumed. My midday nap in the bunkroom followed by time spent sitting at the edge of the pond. I felt my languid body settle more firmly into the ground where I sat as I stared down the side trail of memory. Who knew if I was even capable of setting a record out here? My next box, in Kent, would be there no matter how long it took me to get to it. I'd given up on the schedule anyway. Now I was just doing my best every day.

"Have you done your best today?"

My voice sounded soft in the velvety-dark forest. I hadn't even meant to speak. Nearby an owl answered for me with a trilling *who cooks for you.* I sat quietly, taking in the rustling of tiny feet followed by the almost imperceptible whoosh of feathers as the owl took flight. I listened to the faint susurration of the leaves as they waltzed with the breeze. The wood was dry and cozy. It hadn't rained there.

"No. I haven't," I answered, getting back to my feet.

~

I'd always found the Berkshires to be pleasant. I enjoyed the way the low mountains interspersed with rural communities and agricultural land. What I did not find pleasant were the flies and the humidity.

"Ugh!" I said, wiping my grimy hand across my face and temporarily displacing the swarm of biting black bugs.

I crossed over the Housatonic River via a road bridge, then turned onto the riverside trail. The afternoon sky was predictably growing dark with ominous thunderheads. Sighing, I swatted at the flies, trekking poles flailing. I passed a couple walking their dog. It seemed like it had been a nonstop parade of road crossings and people all across the state. At least after the next highway I'd be heading toward the border with Connecticut. I needed to get across the state line before I slept or I wouldn't have a chance of making it to Kent the following day.

"I'm running low on snacks," I observed, digging in my pack pockets for something to eat.

I chomped exaggeratedly—it was hard to chew my energy blocks without water, and I was out again. It seemed like I could never drink enough water. Yet I also peed constantly. At the next stream I filtered some water, plopped an electrolyte tablet in, and started walking while it fizzed. It was still approximately thirteen miles to the Connecticut border—and camping was forbidden there. Instead, my goal was to reach the far side of Bear Mountain, two and a half miles into Connecticut. I swigged the fizzy water. Despite drinking electrolyte drinks twice a day I simply wasn't getting enough.

"I'm basically a margarita glass," I said, rubbing my temples hard to remove the salt crystals built up along the hairline.

I crossed dirt Jug End Road and threw my pack on the ground before filling my water bottles, again, from the small trickle flowing nearby. When I was finished, I stared at the salt-stained, reeking backpack with disdain. The last thing I wanted to do was put it back on, climb up Jug End, and follow its ascending ridge. I'd hiked thirteen and a half hours already and—aside from two previous water stops—I'd been on the move the entire time. I sat down next to my sweat-soaked pack in the middle of the trail and pulled out a bag of chips and the baggie of salt I'd bought at the Stop & Shop. Leaning back against the slope, I stared up at the gently swaying trees. A few sprinkles made their way through the canopy. I ate the chips ravenously—dousing each one with additional salt. At the sound of voices coming toward me, I tilted my chin back down to see two men hiking southbound.

I sighed and sat up. After pouring the last of the chip crumbs into my mouth, I jumped to my feet as they reached the road. I didn't want to be behind them. Or be seen lying down. I rolled my eyes at my own hubris.

"Hey!" one of them called.

I paused and glanced back, not sure whether he was hailing me or not.

"Anish, right?"

"Um, yeah."

"Wow! Awesome!"

I smiled. I never knew exactly what to say. I was much better at melting into the wilderness than I was at making small talk as a trail celebrity.

"I'm Roamin' and this is Dorito. Are you trying to set the record out here?"

"Nice to meet you. Yeah, I am."

"Incredible! We don't want to slow you down, but mind if we hike with you?"

"Uh, sure."

Roamin' had already reached me on the trail and, as soon as I acquiesced to company, he took off up the switchbacks. I raced after him and Dorito fell into place behind me. I wasn't sure if he was pushing harder than normal because of me or not, but I was swept up in a pace far faster than I would have hiked left to my own tired legs. Roamin' and Dorito peppered me with questions and stories as we hiked and I focused so much on their conversation I forgot my fatigue. Before I knew it, we were crossing the open ledges of Mount Bushnell and beginning our descent into the forest. The pace set by fresher feet had made the dreaded ascent fly by.

My feet skittered around on the wet rocks of the ledges—none of us could see anything through the foggy rain. Once again, I noticed the lack of tread on my battered shoes. I was so glad I would be getting new ones in Kent tomorrow.

"This is where we're camping," Roamin' said, halting at the turnoff to Hemlock shelter.

"But it's only seven," I blurted.

Dorito laughed, "We aren't setting a record!"

"Thanks for hiking with us!" Roamin' added.

"Thank you," I said, and I meant it. With them I'd covered the distance at three miles per hour—unheard of for me after I passed the twelve-hour mark.

"Good luck!" they said, waving as they turned down the spur trail.

I took a deep breath and began the ascent of Mount Everett at a much slower pace. As I hiked I ate cookies with salt thrown on them—they were delicious. *I'm going to have to put salt on every single thing I eat from now on.*

The ongoing rain didn't lower the humidity at all. If anything, it intensified it. Even on the open slab tops of Mounts Everett and Race the air was not moving. I pulled my dress up and tucked it into my waistband. I was still decently covered, but the freshly exposed skin on my upper thigh increased the surface area for evaporating sweat. I longed for night. It seemed like another lifetime ago I'd feared it. Since southern Vermont the crepuscular hours onward were my only relief from insects and humidity, the only time when I felt even remotely comfortable moving. I glanced at my watch. It would be dark before I reached the river at the bottom of Sages Ravine. *At least the climb up Bear Mountain will be in the less humid overnight hours.* Although, its scrambly terrain would be challenging to follow without the sun.

"Nothing I can't handle," I said, thinking not-so-fondly of Maine.

Inky shadows infiltrated the hardwood and hemlock groves and I felt the tension in my body soften. With other hikers safely tucked into tents and shelters, I was at last alone with my fellow creatures of the forest. I pulled my dress even higher and walked faster down into the coolness of Sages Ravine—and the Connecticut-Massachusetts border. When I reached the river crossing, I put my pack on the ground and pulled off my dress. I swirled it in the water—wringing it out away from the creek— and repeated the process, freeing the fabric of salt and dirt. The burbling of the river comforted me as did the feel of the evening air on my naked body. I kicked my shoes off and stepped into the black water. Ripples illuminated by the light of my headlamp shimmered copper. The tannins of the East Coast waterways never ceased to fascinate me. I lowered my body into the iced tea.

I waded back out and briefly debated hiking sans clothes, but decided I was refreshed enough after my dip. I got dressed and crossed the river. *Only a mile to the border....* A few minutes later I was startled by a dog barking. A tent was pitched on the edge of the trail.

"Sorry," I said quietly.

"Oh, sorry! Shh. Sorry." The disembodied woman's voice mixed apology with admonitions to her dog. "I didn't think anyone would be coming through so late."

"It's ok," I said, glad I hadn't decided to hike naked.

I reached the summit of Bear Mountain at eleven. The sky was crystal clear and I leaned against a rock, tilting my face up to take in the sparkling universe. In the wild dark, far away from the light pollution of cities, the stars seemed close enough to touch. I couldn't help but try to pull their energy into my bone-weary body. The many pit stops of my first full day in Massachusetts had slowed me. Kent was thirty-eight miles away and I was down to 1,000 calories in my pack. I briefly debated making the side trip into Salisbury seven miles ahead, but dismissed it. In 2003 I'd hiked nearly all of Connecticut—fifty miles—in a day, with almost no food and no idea what it would be like to travel that far in one day.

"Although you didn't have to do it by 6 p.m.," I reminded myself, thinking of the closing time at the shop where my box waited.

In fact, I'd slept on a rock for a few hours just shy of the fifty-mile mark and finished the distance in the pre-dawn light. It had taken me a full twenty-four hours, including a nap, but I'd done it. My sense of accomplishment had been drowned out by incredible exhaustion, and when I'd reached the Brassie Brook shelter I'd collapsed on the floorboards until noon.

I passed the turnoff to that same shelter at midnight. I imagined I could hear the Salisbury clock bells chiming twelve, as I did in 2003 when I was headed up the mountain toward this very spot. *How things have changed in the intervening years.* I'd been so naive about the toll big miles would take. After running out of food, I'd staggered for two days to reach Upper Goose Pond shelter, where I'd consumed over a dozen pancakes. Now I was here again, in the pitch dark, low on food, but not in any danger of running out. And, unlike the earliest days of my hike, I was simply moving through the night toward my next resupply without the desperation to make miles.

Something had shifted inside me since my sob-fest near the summit of Killington. Now I was hiking songbird to screech owl every day because it felt good to do so. When I crawled into my sleeping bag, I didn't record how far I'd gone because it didn't really matter much anymore. I knew that I was doing my best every day, going until I was simply too dead on my feet to keep putting one in front of the other. I knew the miles would amass from the sheer number of hours I spent moving. Relinquishing the stress of expectations to the universe allowed me to experience nothing but the joy, mixed with pain, of pushing my body to its limit as I crossed the country.

~

I checked my watch again. It still had not been a full hour since my last snack. My stomach roared.

"Fifteen more minutes," I responded.

I tried to wipe sweat off of my face with the back of my hand, but it was too slick with its own perspiration. I pulled up the neckline of my dress and used that. It too was soaked, but I managed to squeegee some of the moisture away. The lower elevations of Connecticut were as muggy as any day I'd spent in the tropics. Little gnats swarmed my eyes and nose. Small trickles of blood oozed from where they'd bitten my hands. I polished off the last of my water. I couldn't drink enough.

"Hi." I was curt to the handful of people perched on rocks and logs near the stream.

They had been chatty when I'd arrived, but when I plunged into the water to fill my bottle they watched me in silence. I was too hot to care. I'd covered twenty miles in seven hours and I still had eighteen to go—plus a mile on the highway—to reach my resupply box in Kent. The store closed at six. If I maintained my pace, I would get there just in time.

Thirty-eight miles in thirteen hours. Ugh.

Once past the stream, I mixed jogging into my stride on the flatter sections of trail. The only way to make it was to move faster.

"I have to move faster," I urged myself breathlessly.

I'd drank nearly a gallon of water and yet I had only peed twice. I thought about the day of blood in Maine. It scared me to think it might happen again. So, I kept adding salt to my food for extra electrolytes and drinking as much as I could. I tried to not think about it happening again. Instead, I thought about how I was nearly out of food, which meant my pack weighed about ten pounds. I was able to pull the straps on my backpack's hipbelt tight and jog without it bouncing wildly. My legs pistoned faster relatively well despite their single-speed usage over the previous weeks.

"I can't miss this box," I told myself sternly as the trail wound up a hill.

I leaned into it, grinding upward at a decidedly uncomfortable pace. If I didn't reach Kent tonight, I would have to camp before the highway and wait until the store opened in the morning. It would cost me even more precious hours—this time not because of an unavoidable natural obstacle, but my own inability to hightail it. I could accept the limitations of rivers more easily than I could accept the limitations of my own body.

My watch beeped. I ate a handful of dried-fruit-and-nut bites doused in salt, and swigged the electrolyte drink I'd made at my last water stop. I was woozy—whether from the heat, humidity, dehydration, or lack of calories, I had no idea. Probably some combination of all of them. I suspected, despite the tablets and salt, that I wasn't consuming enough electrolytes. After all, I was soaked in sweat from eight in the morning to eight in the evening every single day.

"I've gotta adapt to this at some point," I gasped.

I crested a hill and headed down yet again. The climbs and descents were shorter in Connecticut than in other places on the trail. No wonder, in my naive early hiking days, I'd believed other hikers when they told me it was "flat." Their assurances had lured me into my first fifty-mile day. Connecticut was by no means flat, but I'd indeed covered those miles. Now here I was running it backward. I'd be in New York in the morning.

The trail intersected dirt River Road and I started running again alongside the broad Housatonic River. I paused at a spring to fill my bottle, chug, and refill. I realized how silly it must seem that I was running and exhausting myself to reach the box. Yet since the night at Upper Goose Pond I'd known I was going to keep pushing. None of my questions about my ability would be answered if I didn't. Each day I awoke at 4 a.m. and moved until my legs wobbled and my eyes could barely focus on the trail tread. Eventually collapse would become inevitable—that was when I would allow myself to stop. I knew that if I focused on reaching that point daily I would have done my best. There was simply nothing more I could do. My absolute best every single day would give me my absolute best result. Regardless of whether it was a record or not, it would be what I could do. I would once and for all be able to define my limits and abilities.

I could feel a hot spot on my left heel growing more intense. I knew I should stop and take care of it. But I needed to get to my box. I'd have new shoes and clean socks. I'd be able to eat ice cream and sit. *God, I want to sit.* I could deal with it in . . .

"Three miles," I encouraged my tired legs.

I looked at my watch—5:05 p.m. I willed myself to move faster as I climbed toward St. Johns Ledges. I remembered how, in August of 2003, I'd found a woman sitting in the woods during the morning hours. I'd been short of breath and angry that Connecticut was not flat after all. The young woman resting on a log, gazing into the thicket, had been a complete surprise. Her beanie was pulled tight around her ears as shafts of sunlight illuminated breath wafting out in clouds. Hot and sweaty from covering twenty miles already, I'd stormed up the trail, high on endorphins and youthful anticipation. She simply sat and stared into the sunbeams streaking down through the canopy.

"Good morning," she greeted me quietly.

"Good morning," I said, slowing down a bit to study her serene face. "Beautiful morning, isn't it?"

She crossed her legs and scooted to the side. Despite my goals for the day, I accepted the invitation to join her and sat down.

"I'm Deer."

"I'm Anish."

She'd pulled a granola bar from her pack and was chewing thoughtfully on it. Realizing I was desperately hungry, I pulled out my lunch.

"Have you hiked here from Georgia?"

"Yes." I took a bite. "You?"

"I'm SoBo. I started in Maine two months ago. There's so much to see out here."

I nodded and continued plowing through my food. Once finished, I stood up and put my pack back on. She didn't look like she planned to move anytime soon.

"Well, have a nice hike. I've got to get going."

"Thank you."

"I'm trying to hike Connecticut in a day—fifty miles," I added awkwardly, by way of explanation for my rapid departure.

"Why?"

The question wasn't new. I'd been hiking thirty-mile days consistently since southern Virginia.

"I want to know if I can do it."

She nodded. "That's why I'm on the trail, too."

I smiled at her and she smiled back. Then I reluctantly left the presence of one of the few female solo hikers I'd ever met. Over the years I'd often wondered whether she reached Springer Mountain.

Sweltering in the New England summer, I passed the spot where I'd met Deer. I could almost feel her quiet presence—a slice of solemn calm in the face of my exuberance. I'd carried her memory with me for twelve years. My energy was still exuberant. I was still wondering if I could do it. Was she?

I reached the highway at 5:48 p.m. I had twelve minutes to run a mile and collect my box. The sound of feet slapping on the pavement and ragged breaths distracted me from how altogether frazzled I was. *I'm going to make it.... I'm going to make it....*

Arriving at the store, I grabbed the door handle and yanked— half expecting it to already be locked. But it opened and I rushed into the combined gift shop and ice cream parlor. Air conditioning bathed me in its refreshing embrace and the smell of coffee drew me to the counter. It was 5:58 p.m.

"Can I help you?" A blonde woman came out of the back. She did not seem perturbed that it was two minutes to closing time.

"Hi, I sent a box here. Heather Anderson."

"Do you want some ice cream?"

"Uh, is there still time?"

She shrugged a bit and smiled. "I'm usually here doing paperwork until quarter after."

"Oh. Yes. Yes, uh…" I stared at the options on the menu board— my mind suddenly mush now that I'd met my sole objective for the day.

"I'll go get your box while you decide."

She came back a few minutes later with my box.

"I'll take the largest chocolate milkshake you can make with a double shot of espresso in it."

A few minutes later I was in a chair in the parking lot with my box and an immense milkshake. I sucked it down blissfully, relishing my only break of the entire day. As I sat, I grew mindful of my body: the throbbing blister on my left foot, the aching soles of my feet, the chafe along my back, armpits, and bra line, the stiffness in my neck from squaring my backpack-laden shoulders. My legs quivered with exhaustion and my skin was flushed and sweaty. Ice cream in the pit of my stomach nestled against my organs, cooling me from the inside. I felt the sugar and caffeine unfurl, spreading their tendrils throughout my bloodstream until at last they tingled the place behind my eyes. I felt as though I could function again.

Bending down, I opened the box and threw its contents into my pack. I ate the treats I'd packed myself for immediate consumption and threw my demolished shoes inside the now-empty box. I started to peel my sock off to swap it for a clean one—underneath I glimpsed the largest blister I'd ever had. The humidity of New England had resulted in a half-golf-ball-sized lump, dwarfing anything I'd acquired in the triple-digit heat of Southern California.

"Oh. My. God."

I rolled the sock back up and slid my sweltering, reeking feet into the soft, unspoiled shoes. It felt so wrong, but I knew that within a day and a half those kicks would be as disgusting as my feet whether I put clean socks on now or later. I disposed of my garbage and headed back to the trail.

With darkness came thunder and the first sprinkles of an impending twenty-four-hour rain. *At least the humidity will break overnight,* I thought. *Perhaps I'll even be able to sleep in my sleeping bag for the first time since Vermont.*

Reaching camp, I pitched my tent. The rain was picking up and I knew I'd be in a deluge soon. Once inside I peeled off my socks and gently rubbed hand sanitizer on the blister, and on a needle from my sewing kit. I pulled the skin taut and inserted the needle into the bubble. Liquid shot out and hit the ceiling of the tent.

"Oh lord," I said as I squeezed it gently, draining fluid, until the tortured skin lay flat and wrinkled like a deflated balloon.

I dabbed triple antibiotic ointment onto the area and slid my feet into my clean socks. Then I worked my compression socks on top of those so they would passively continue the draining process while I slept. Thunder gave way to pouring rain as I gave way to sleep.

RAIN OR SHINE

IT WAS STILL RAINING when I woke up at four, and judging by the depth of the puddles outside, it had rained nonstop since I fell asleep. I made my way up the moonless trail, moving slowly in the dark. It took several miles to work the stiffness that had accumulated while I slept out of my body, and the chilly downpour made it take even longer. I flirted with the border of Connecticut and New York, weaving through pastures and forests until I crossed the road near Bull's Bridge. I expected the rain to relent as the day warmed, but the temperature remained constant. Climbing Ten Mile Hill I sweated into my rain jacket and poncho, only to grow cold and clammy as I made my way down the other side. Finally, I crossed Hoyt Road, entering New York.

My blistered heel was raw from incessantly rubbing against my wet shoe. The silver lining—if it could be considered one— was that my new socks and shoes were still clean, since the rainfall was washing the mud off as quickly as it accumulated. Unfortunately, even that didn't last. Soon mucky water was oozing into my shoes as I traversed cow pastures and climbed over fences on rickety stiles. I cringed thinking of the bacterial bath my open wound was immersed in.

My mind wandered while I hiked, as it was prone to do during the long, lonesome hours on trail. When it tired of trail math—calculating the distance to water, calories in my pack, and elevation change—it moved on to more ponderous problems, such as why trees always fell across the trail at heights that made it difficult to cross them and whether or not backpacking could permanently alter my posture.

Bored of all of that, my thoughts began to swirl around memories. Memories of beautiful, wondrous moments as well as time with family and friends. Most days, the inevitable course of my thoughts would then lead to all the things I'd ever done wrong. The cringeworthy moments and the helpless ones. Times when I'd been angry, and others when I'd been embarrassed.

My mood sank into those deeper realms as I sloshed along the trail. This time it wandered to rainy spring days in Michigan. I thought of the brand-new kite that my dad and I had taken out on a blustery April afternoon. We'd struggled to get it aloft, the winds were so high. Once it was finally soaring, I'd fought to control it despite my dad's instructions. Inevitably, the kite had plummeted to the ground—smashing into pieces. My dad had been so angry, and I'd sobbed. I was surprised that even now I felt sadness thinking about my kite-flying failure when I was seven years old.

"Thank goodness," I said aloud as the afternoon sun at last broke through the clouds.

The sudden brightness made me squint as I descended a pasture toward Route 22. More than sadness, I realized that the hollowness in my gut—that told me I was a fluke, inadequate—was the same hollowness I felt thinking about my smashed kite. I had never been good at any sport. I'd smashed my kite, but I'd also been unable to ice skate, play baseball, hit a golf ball, or do anything else my dad had tried to teach me. I'd never been good enough. My mom had always comforted me after these failures while I cried. She'd always told me that it didn't matter if I was athletic. I was a great writer. My gifts were elsewhere.

I gulped deep breaths of the clean country air. It was hard to believe there was a train station down the road that could take you directly into the heart of NYC. I felt warm as I let go of a pain that had weighed me down for so long. A pain I hadn't even known I'd held. *I'm not an uncoordinated child anymore.* Sparkling grass lifted my mood in the way only sunshine after rain can. I crossed over Route 22 and headed for the hiker-friendly plant nursery a few yards off trail. A sign there directed me to a faucet and hose near the back fence where I refilled my water bottles, grateful for the business's generosity to hikers.

I stripped my socks off and rinsed them and my feet thoroughly. Then I wrung the socks out, lavished triple antibiotic ointment on the painful, red blister, and slid the socks back on. I hoped the antibiotic would do its job and keep me free from infection. Ready to hike again, I returned to the AT and hustled across the slippery planks of the boardwalk over the Swamp River. I continued weaving through pastures, across bogs adorned with cattails, and along muddy dirt trails as the sun played peekaboo with me. Rain would fall, pause just enough to nurture false hope, and then fall again even harder. I reached the eerily quiet environs of Nuclear Lake and tried to hurry around it. I couldn't jog now that I had three days of food on my back, but I was happy the trail was flat and easy. In 2003 I'd been shot at—or so it had seemed since the sound was so loud—as I'd rounded the head of Nuclear Lake. Back then I'd hit the ground and army crawled a short distance in the dirt before jumping to my feet and running my little heart out. Today I was too weary—not to mention sore—from my flight across Connecticut to move any quicker than a brisk walk. The area had been deemed safe for public use after the plutonium research facility was closed, but it remained ominous to me. I was grateful to be past it and moving steadily away.

~

A couple of mornings later, as I made my way up slabby trail in the early light, I allowed my mind to wander further afield. I was nearly eight hundred miles into the hike. Already 3,000 calories per day felt like barely enough, mainly because it was taking more days than planned to reach each new resupply box. Originally the box I picked up in Kent was supposed to last me three days, as I traveled across the remainder of Connecticut, all of New York, and all of New Jersey. I was already on day two and I was not going to reach New Jersey until evening. It would be a longer than normal day across the state to reach my next box at the Delaware Water Gap by nightfall. I reminded myself I was consuming far more than I had on the PCT and therefore had no reason to use limited calories as an excuse for my pace. *But that trail is easier.*

I'd been an overweight child and teen. From an early age I'd starved myself, sometimes subsisting on nothing but baby carrots until—inevitably—I would break down and binge. It was always a sign of weakness, as I told my reflection in the mirror. *You're fat. You're ugly. No one will ever love you.* I repeated these vituperations over and over.

How many hours of my life had I spent telling myself I was fat? Thru-hiking had provided a pathway out of that cycle. The wilderness did not care how I looked. The trail showed me that I was not an overweight, clumsy child. I was capable of difficult physical feats and, to do them, I needed fuel. I smiled thinking of the gluten-free pizza I'd ordered the day before, at a gas station a stone's throw from the AT north of Bear Mountain Park. It had lasted approximately five minutes. The pint of ice cream for dessert had lasted a hair less. But despite having broken my disordered eating cycle, I was still scarred by my own words. *Will I ever be good enough for myself?*

"Watch out!"

I leaped to the side of the trail—nearly losing my balance—at the sound of the man yelling. He careened past me at breakneck speed—on a unicycle. I stood panting with my hand over my heart and turned to see him disappear down the smooth rocks. My watch beeped and I pulled a baggie of M&M's out of my pack's side pocket. I threw a giant handful in my mouth and resumed climbing—cautiously.

"If you find yourself eating M&M's at 7 a.m., hopefully you are thru-hiking or running an ultra," I told the now-empty trail. "Otherwise, you may need an intervention. Also, if you almost get run over by a backcountry unicyclist that early, you've got to be in New York."

I shook my head as my heart rate returned to its usual beats per minute, my wandering thoughts derailed onto another set of tracks. The mobs of people swarming the trail as it passed through Bear Mountain State Park the day before, and the absolute absurdity of following white blazes through a bona fide zoo—complete with bears and a reptile house—somehow helped normalize the oddity of the man on one wheel who'd nearly run me over. I remembered the look of sadness in the bear's eyes as I passed its cage. I was freer than it would ever be and that seemed damned unfair.

Soon storm clouds began to pile up. The excess moisture on the ground from the round-the-clock rain a few days prior had proved fodder enough to build new storms earlier in the day. As they grew, evaporation swelled the moisture content of the air so that it seemed as though I could simply walk with my mouth open and quench my thirst. *Unfortunately, the water cycle doesn't work that way.* I paused on the summit of Mombasha

High Point and looked at the next several road crossings in my Awol guide.

"Heaven Hill Farm," I said out loud, skimming the entry of the business a stone's throw from the trail at the Route 94 crossing near Vernon, New Jersey.

I did some quick math. I'd be there in the late afternoon or early evening. Hours weren't listed, but snacks and ice cream were. I put the pages away and kept hiking, following the undulating ridgeline.

"Don't get your hopes up," I warned myself. "You don't know the hours."

Despite my own admonition, it was impossible *not* to get my hopes up. I desperately wanted to eat ice cream, drink soda, and consume whatever else the farm might have for me. I scrambled up and down the rocky outcrops and slabs as I drew ever closer to the state line. The clouds matured and wrung themselves out, leaving me to slip and skid on the wet rocks, falling over and over again.

"Just slow down, Anish," I told myself after the third fall resulted in a bloody knee. "Either they'll be open or they won't. Breaking your bones isn't going to do you any good at all."

A streak of lightning made me jump and scurry despite my own chiding. At last I reached the rock with "NY/NJ" spray-painted in white. I snapped a quick picture and scrambled down off of the long ridgeline into the trees, relieved to be away from the lightning and pummeling rain.

I crossed the shoulder of hulking Wawayanda Mountain at 5 p.m. From there, I was only two miles from Heaven Hills Farm. Descending, I was surprised at the number of people on the AT heading down the mountain. My feet had become agile predictors of landing angles after eight hundred miles of ceaseless negotiation, and I jockeyed around them as they tentatively picked their way across the rocks.

"Must be a popular day-hiking area," I murmured to myself as I darted around yet another large group near the bottom of the mountain where the trail widened and flattened.

I burst into the open, taking in the rolling pastures and farm stand a short distance up the road. Then I jogged toward the packed parking lot, holding my breath. It was 5:45 p.m. I reached the door and exhaled—a sign said they were open until six.

"Hello!" a woman sweeping the floor cheerfully greeted me when I stepped inside.

"Hi! I'm so glad you're open."

"For a few more minutes anyway."

"I won't take long."

I turned in a circle, honing in on the essentials: coffee, ice cream, and fresh popped caramel kettle corn. I grabbed a large Styrofoam coffee cup and filled it to the brim. At the scoop counter I carefully studied the bins of ice cream.

"Hard to choose, huh?" said the woman, setting down her broom and slipping on gloves.

"Can I get it in a bowl? I can't eat cones."

"Of course. One or two scoops?"

"Two. Coffee and chocolate, please."

She glanced at the steaming cup in my hands and smiled as she began to scoop the coffee ice cream into a dish.

"Long day?"

"Very. And it's not over yet."

"Well, I think this stop will help," she said, piling an extra scoop onto the already gigantic pile and handing it across the counter.

"Thank you!"

"Sure thing. You can eat at the tables outside when you're ready. There's a trash can and a faucet out there too."

I darted around the food section of the store, gathering bars and a bag of trail mix into the hem of my skirt while still balancing the towering ice cream and the twenty-ounce coffee. I paused in front of the produce—longing for the vegetables—and couldn't resist grabbing a pint of berries and a block of farm fresh cheese. Finally, I waddled over to the register and unloaded my skirt onto the belt.

"I'm sorry it took me so long. So many options."

"It's just six now. You're fine. Would you like a bag?"

"No, that's not necessary. I don't want to waste one."

"How about one of these?" She plopped a plastic shopping basket onto the counter. "You can leave it right outside the door."

"That would be perfect. Thank you."

By 6:15, I'd consumed the berries, ice cream, and coffee as well as nibbled the cheese and caramel corn. I was dismayed to see that in my zeal I'd bought a bag as tall as my small backpack. With my food bag already swollen with the new additions, there was simply no room for the caramel corn.

Oh, no! What have you done, Anish? I wondered to myself.

I fiddled with the package and the straps, trying to see if I could rig some sort of feed bag. Finally, I managed to attach the caramel corn at an angle under my left armpit where I could eat with my right hand while walking. I headed across the field toward the mile-long Pochuck Boardwalk, and sped across the swamplands on deserted, flat, and—thankfully—dry slats while gobbling caramel corn. I flew up the ascent south of County Road 517 and through the rolling hills beyond, fueled by sugar and caffeine.

"New Jersey is FLAT. I'm cruising!" I crowed.

I felt flooded with happiness. For the first time on the entire hike I felt a true glimmer of hope: I might be able to complete the task before me.

~

The quadfecta high of sugar, caffeine, calories, and easy trail didn't last. It was pitch-black by the time I reached paved and deserted Liberty Corners Road. I'd gone from jubilant to melancholy and sluggish. I ate some candy, hoping to bring my blood sugar back into equilibrium before reaching the circuitous route that traced a near square around the Wallkill River National Wildlife Refuge. The trail was two miles long and flat, but decidedly empty of humanity. The only sounds were soft splashes of what I hoped were waterfowl, not water snakes or wading bears in the unseen swamps. My breath rose in clouds around me as I hoofed it at top speed. Many eyes—of the animals who called this place home— followed me through the darkness. When I finally reached the road walk on State Line Road, I was relieved to be away from the eldritch wetland.

As I crossed the Wallkill River and turned onto Carnegie Road, I finally felt the hairs that had pricked on the back of my neck begin to settle. I moved once again into the patchwork of hardwood groves and fields that comprised the bulk of the Appalachian Trail across northern New Jersey.

The roads and trail danced together in a close embrace for several miles along the New Jersey-New York border. As I neared Quarry Road the still night was shattered by the roar of an engine a short distance away, followed by a loud bang, squealing tires, and men's voices whooping. Instinctively I hastened my pace, bolting across the road. No sooner had I made myself invisible in the trail's brush than I heard the car flooring it back toward me. More yelling. Another bang. I ran.

"Hey! What's that light down there?"

I froze at the sound of the man's clearly audible voice. They had seen my headlamp. Without thinking I hit the ground, covering my light with my open palm. I fumbled to click it off as the car slowed to a prowl a few hundred feet away. *Do they know about the AT?* I wondered. *What would they do if they found me here, alone, in the middle of the night?* My stomach knotted itself—I could guess what might happen. I lay there with my nose pressed against the dirt, breathing in the rich humus smell and noting the scratchiness of grass on my cheeks, legs, and arms. The car was still close. I lifted myself onto my hands and toes—bear crawling forward with my light off. I could see the illumination of the headlights above me. I worried that if I stood, the men would see me.

"Ain't nothing over there, dipshit." The car peeled away.

I got to my feet and ran without turning my headlamp on. A quarter mile later I saw the glow of a lone streetlight illuminating an intersection. Ducking behind a tree marked in white, I willed myself to melt into the shadows. I struggled to breathe quietly as I rested my head against the rough bark just below the blaze, listening to the dense silence. I peered around the trees. The roads were as empty as rural roads should be at that hour.

"Just Saturday night shenanigans," I whispered to myself encouragingly.

I crept to the edge of the road, ready to flee backward into the lightless forest if necessary. Checking both directions, I neither saw—nor heard—anything. I had no idea how the roads connected. Perhaps they didn't and the trail had taken me far from the men and their joyriding. Across the street I spied the white blaze marking a narrow trail into the woods. I took a deep breath to try and quell the shaking in my hands, then I bolted.

For what seemed like an eternity I was vulnerable on the blacktop, illumined by the orange glow of a single street light. Then I was back in the shadows and moving fast. Tripping over unseen obstacles, my extinguished headlamp impuissant to stop my foundering. Screeching tires, shouting, the emphatic revving of an engine overwhelmed my ears. I fled in a panic until I crossed a gravel driveway half a mile later. I knew the road must still be very close, but in another half a mile I would come to the drive leading to the Secret shelter, cabins and campsites situated on private land. I would be safe there. I clicked on my light and continued to run.

Reaching the turnoff, I swung right and ran a quarter mile down the road—back into New York. The moonlight illumined a clearing with a couple of small cabins and I slowed to a walk. I could see a handful of tents pitched on the lawn. There were probably a dozen hikers there. *I'm safe.*

I shuffled across the dewy grass to a tree far from everyone else. After pitching my tent with trembling fingers, I crawled inside at midnight. I lay there after I ate, staring at the moon through the wispy fabric of my tent. I was enervated from the day and yet innervated by my brush with the most formidable animal.

~

The miles passed faster than usual, and yet time still dragged on. New Jersey was essentially one continuous ridgeline, and it was fifty miles from the Secret shelter to the Pennsylvania border on the Delaware River. *Shouldn't I be walking over three miles per hour?* Yet the lack of elevation gain and loss was more than made up for in the uneven rockiness of the tread itself. *I thought the rocks weren't supposed to get bad until Pennsylvania?!* I knew I should know better. The entire Appalachian Trail was rocky. Either you scrambled up and down giant blocky boulders for miles on end, or you contended with broken slab and jagged talus constantly affecting your footing and pace. The southern Appalachians were the most forgiving . . . but I was still very far from there.

For what I presumed was an appropriate amount of time due a lackluster state high point, I stood on the deck of the High Point Observation Tower and admired the slightly higher forested hill—adorned with an obelisk—a half mile off trail. I threw a handful of cacao nibs in my mouth and descended the steps back to the AT.

"I hope I find water soon," I muttered.

Everything was dry—every damn stream and spring. The stinking bogs were still flush with fetid water, but there was no way I would drink from them. The rocky spine I traveled was not only an impediment to my progress but also to proper hydration. "This is why most people do the Jersey Challenge," I grumbled. From my first thru-hike in 2003 I remembered that nearly everyone's goal was to eat breakfast, lunch, and dinner in the many towns only a few miles off trail. Already thirty-two miles into my day, I had no time for extra mileage or stops: I was nearly out of food, and I still needed to cover the twenty-eight miles to Delaware Water Gap to reach my box. There was a church hostel there as well, which made it the obvious choice for that night's destination. My body had adapted as much as it would. It was time to try and reel in the miles and hours lost in Maine and New Hampshire.

I'd been out of water for nearly two hours when I finally reached the highway passing through Culvers Gap. Water and food beckoned. I hastened toward the lone building on the other side of the roadway called the AT Deli and opened the door.

"Pack outside!" the man at the counter yelled.

I stopped in the doorway, shocked.

"Uh, can I get water here?"

"No. Pack outside!" He came out from behind the counter, obviously angry.

"Ok. Sorry."

I stepped back, closing the door. I stared at it. There wasn't a sign requesting packs be left outside. I wondered why he was so angry. *How should I know?* The Awol guide said the deli was a hiker-friendly store where you could get water, drinks, and food. *Obviously not anymore.* I went to the edge of the parking lot and pulled out my phone. I desperately wanted to go in and buy some food, but I was too scared. The Guthook app finally loaded and I scrolled through the upcoming waypoints, trying to decide where the next water was.

"Gyp's is a quarter mile that way."

I looked up to see that the man had followed me outside and was standing in front of the door, pointing toward the town of Branchville and Gyp's Tavern—the opposite way of the trail. Everything in his demeanor demanded I leave the premises.

I didn't say anything. I spun around and ran for the bushes where the AT ascended up and away from the road. Once out of sight I continued to study the app for potential water sources. There might be a spring at the Brink Road shelter four miles ahead. *And a quarter mile off trail, straight downhill.* I sighed and headed uphill—back to the high and dry ridge.

My heart sank when I was still several yards away from the turnoff to the shelter. I could see a piece of paper flapping on the signpost. I knew what it said, but I still stopped to confirm.

"Spring is dry."

My throat was too dry to even speak out loud. I moved my lips, barely whispering, as I read it. It was another six miles to the Blue Mountain Trailhead and the spring there. Nearly five hours would have passed since I last had water by the time I got there. I hoped it was flowing. *I've been through worse.* In the triple-digit heat of the southern Pacific Crest Trail I'd never been able to gauge how much I would drink or whether sources would be dry. The heat index here was probably in the nineties, but I knew that I would survive. *As long as I don't start bleeding again.*

The Appalachian Trail circled high above New Jersey's diminutive Crater Lake. A few hundred feet below me I could hear the sounds of people splashing. The water glimmered in the sun, beckoning. *I'm so thirsty.* It was still two miles to the spring at the trailhead and an equally far detour out and back to the lake below. I was also ravenous. I'd skipped the last two snacks because, without water, I couldn't swallow . . . or digest.

After what felt like an eternity, I reached a gravel road and turned right. Realizing my error when I found no spring, I went back to the intersection, turned left, and arrived at a parking lot. Nothing. I felt a sense of urgent panic rising inside me.

"I need water!" My voice rasped on the words.

I spun around and walked back to the trail. I looked at the woods I'd emerged from. There was a tiny sign pointing toward the parking lot: "Water .1"

I retraced my steps to the parking lot. Of course, the sign was oriented for northbounders. *Southbounders don't get signs. They just have to figure it out.* Irritated, I marched past the parking lot and down to a metal gate across the road. *This is .1, now where is it?* I stood there for a moment and listened. My ears slowly adjusted to the humidity-soaked quietude. A squirrel scuffled to my left and a bird chirped in a tree behind me. There was also the nearly imperceptible murmur of moving water. I ran down the road beyond the gate. As I came around the bend, I saw a muddy stain running across the gravel. Black tubing protruded from the ground in a patch of trees above the road. Clear, cool water gushed out of it steadily. I scanned the area for snakes before getting down on my knees. I lowered my mouth to the stream gushing from the tube and let it fill, swallow . . . repeat.

I sat back, filled my bottle, and dropped an electrolyte tablet in. While it dissolved I filled my water bladder. I downed the electrolytes, refilled, and drank more. My belly was distended with the volume of icy fluid, and I remembered the time when—dangerously dehydrated—I'd chugged too much cold spring water on the PCT and nearly passed out. I dumped a bottle of water over my head, gasping at the delightful shiver that ran through me. Leaning back on my pack, I pulled out my three-hour backlog of snacks and wolfed them down.

"Not much left," I muttered, staring into my nearly empty food bag.

After a much needed ten minutes on my butt, I got up and headed back toward the trail. My stomach and pack sloshed, but my feet felt light. It was late afternoon and still nineteen miles to the hostel in Delaware Water Gap, Pennsylvania, but at least now I felt like I could make it there.

The Appalachian Trail in other states meandered through forests, taking acute routes up and down mountains. In New Jersey, however, it seemed abnormally intent on taking a direct path. Barreling along the intermittently open ridge toward the ever-closer halfway point in Pennsylvania, I felt as though I was striding the rooftop of the East. Above me was nothing but thin tree cover and the endless cerulean bowl of sky—a sky steadily clotting with creamy clouds the heat waves whipped into meringue peaks.

"I am so sick of thunderstorms," I sighed.

My dress was soggy with sweat and the fibers were rough with salt. Rain would at least wash away some of the abrasive crystals, but then again, the wet fabric would chafe me all the same. My arms were blotched with heat rash and my blistered feet rubbed from the moisture of sweaty feet. There was simply no escaping water in its undrinkable form.

I heard the first grumble of thunder as I began to descend from Kittatinny Ridge. The sound was distant, yet ominous. I crossed a road and began to ascend again onto Raccoon Ridge. It wouldn't be dusk for another hour, yet the clouds had already begun to obscure the sun. My body—attuned to the sun's circadian rhythm—felt displaced from the passage of time by the premature dimming of the sky. I checked my app. It was five miles to the glacial tarn, Sunfish Pond, from where the trail descended rapidly to the Delaware River, over 1,000 feet below. Until then, I would be exposed on an open ridgeline of slabby rock.

My vantage encompassed sweeping views of the mountainous Poconos and Delaware River drainage as well as the ridges and valleys of New Jersey and eastern Pennsylvania. Ordinarily I would have reveled in the expansive tableaus; however, they also meant vulnerability to the growing number of lightning strikes. I couldn't help but jump every time a crack of thunder rang out. As I raced toward the forests surrounding Sunfish Pond—still nearly two miles distant—the wind rose. For the first time on the entire hike I felt the vapor release from my skin and clothing. Each time I left the sparse cover of trees for another open area, I lost my balance in the face of the gale.

"It's about to get worse," I whispered to myself as I looked westward, fighting to stay on my feet by planting my poles forcefully.

What had once been a sea of marshmallow puffs bobbing in a violaceous sky was now a battalion of fierce clouds approaching swiftly. A deluge of water accompanied by the utter expunction of light hit me like a tsunami and I gasped at its sudden force. I felt as though I would drown simply by breathing. The wind intensified even more, knocking me off my feet. I rolled on the slippery rocks, jockeying for purchase to stop myself. I managed to get back up and fight my way toward the protective embrace of a few stunted trees. Once there, I squatted down and hastened to get my headlamps and poncho out of my pack. My defenders bent low over me in the face of the tempest. Frequent lightning illuminated my world in bursts, leaving me temporarily blinded each time. I battled to get the poncho on as the wind thwarted my efforts. At last I succeeded and was fighting my way forward again—the trail lit by my headlamps and my body sheltered by a thin sheet of wind-whipped plastic.

I reached a stand of sturdy trees marking the beginning of the short descent toward Sunfish Pond. Finally safe from the climactic assault, I breathed a sigh of relief. Unfortunately, my relief lasted just a few minutes. Though the trees above me were bigger, they were no less affected than the smaller ones on top of the ridge. The timber danced jerkily in its waltz with the squall. Branches broke and plummeted to the ground, shaking the earth. One struck the trail in front of me and impaled itself deep into the sodden soil. I shrieked and skidded to a halt, only to watch the five-foot-long limb tip and fall away from me in slow motion—spraying wet clumps of dirt as its buried end dislodged itself from its shallow grave. I fought my way through the wet leaves and over the bulk of the detached bough.

I ran until I reached the shore of Sunfish Pond. Again in the open, the dazzling light show in the otherwise inky sky was clearly visible. Bolts smashed into the landscape around me. The pond itself seethed in a frenzy of sable waves. The monsoon had not relented in the slightest since it had begun an hour before—now the tarn was escaping its rocky embankments and submerging the faint trail that wove through the talus. I strained to spot the blazes painted on the rocks as I circled the pond. My pace slowed to a crawl as I waded through ankle-deep water, picking my way along the broken terrain. I tried desperately not to think about the vast number of water snakes that called the pond home.

A half mile later I was finally freed from the difficult footing when the path left the shore and widened, reflecting the popularity of this section of trail. I passed a deserted backpacker campsite and sped through Worthington State Forest, still deafened by thunder and dodging falling tree limbs.

"Finally!" I exclaimed as the trail began to drop elevation in earnest.

A few minutes later the wail of air sirens drowned out the storm. In my Midwestern upbringing that sound meant one thing: tornado.

I panicked and ran again.

Nine hundred vertical feet lower, the rain slowed to a drizzle and I slowed to a walk, my adrenaline and calories nearly depleted. The trees retired from their tango as the thunder receded into the distance—replaced with the faint hum of

Interstate 80 ahead of me. Soon I was at the empty Dunnfield Creek Trailhead and the rain stopped altogether. I followed the blazes painted on the roadway across a quiet I-80 and onto an empty bike path. To my left the Delaware River moved strong and slow, unaffected by the havoc of the weather. Here the summer night felt abidingly calm after the chaos. I moved rapidly with the last of the adrenaline ebbing out of my bloodstream, uncertain about how safe a deserted bike path along an interstate in the middle of the night was.

The weight of the fifty miles I'd covered on only four hours of sleep settled in my bones as I trod high above the river on a bridge. I reached where the words Pennsylvania and New Jersey were spray-painted on the deck at the invisible midline of the river. As I stepped from one state to the next, my watch beeped: midnight.

HALFWAY

SEVEN STATES DOWN, SEVEN TO GO. I stared at the daylight permeating the ceiling of my tent for a few minutes before glancing down at my watch: it was seven in the morning. The outfitter holding my box wouldn't open for three more hours, yet I was wide awake now, my mind telling me I had overslept. I willed myself into a seated position and got dressed. After quickly striking camp I surveyed the area—I hadn't been able to see my campsite while setting up after midnight.

The church hostel had changed a lot since I'd been there in 2003. The wide-open yard where hikers tented seemed smaller. There were multiple new structures, including a three-sided shelter identical to those found on the trail. I walked over to the bunkroom in the main building. On the door was a single page: "BOIL WATER ADVISORY IN EFFECT."

"You've got to be kidding me."

It had been eight hundred miles since my last—and only—shower of the hike in Monson, Maine. Finally, after all the humidity and mud, a shower was available. And the water was unsafe. Not to mention that I hadn't bothered to refill my water or drink much of anything since the storm caught me the night before. Now my body was reminding me I'd covered fifty broiling miles on only a few liters. Frustrated, I yanked the door open and stepped inside.

Hikers were sleeping on every available bunk and couch. Gear was strewn on every surface. I gingerly stepped over their things and wound my way past inert bodies. Another sign advising me not to drink the water hung on the bathroom door. *I'll keep my mouth shut like I did in Mexico.* I resolutely closed the door, locked it, and turned the hot water in the shower on full blast.

It's impossible to describe the bliss of a scalding shower on skin coated in weeks of sweat and dirt. I shampooed my hair three times, all the while holding my mouth and nose out of the spray. I soaped and rinsed, soaped and rinsed, sending chocolate-brown water swirling around my feet and down the drain. I lathered shampoo into my once white floral-print dress and rinsed it. I wrung it out and repeated. Now cream colored, it once again looked and felt like soft fabric rather than something laced with itchy fiberglass.

Wringing out the sopping garment and strapping it to the outside of my backpack, I dried off and put on my fleece sleeping clothes, which smelled only marginally better than the dress had. I made my way carefully out of the bunkhouse and into the yard. I consulted the Awol guide for food options since there were still over two hours to kill. A quarter of a mile down the road, just beyond the Edge of the Woods Outfitter, was a small restaurant.

The streets were empty. It was Sunday after all. *Yet another reason not to be in my tent when the churchgoers arrive.* My stomach growled loud enough that the squirrel on the sidewalk ahead of me noticed and scampered toward a tree. I reached the restaurant and found my way to a booth near the door.

"Coffee?" the waitress asked, appearing at my table.

"Yes. Please."

"Some storm last night," she commented, pouring me a mug of steaming caffeine.

"Tell me about it. I was hiking in it."

"Oh my! That late?"

"Yeah, I just wanted to get to town. Lightning was striking all over up by Sunfish."

She shook her head. "Glad you're safe. Know what you want?"

"I'll take the biggest breakfast you have."

She laughed and reached for the menu.

"Can I hold on to it?" I asked.

She laughed even harder. "Sure."

She refilled the coffee twice more before I'd finished plowing through the bacon, eggs, sausage, and home fries.

"Anything else? Another cup of coffee?"

"Sure! And, how about the breakfast hash?"

"You got it."

At ten to ten I unplugged my phone from the wall and waddled out of the restaurant. After four cups of coffee, two breakfasts, and a shower I felt strong and revitalized. I reached the outfitter as a brunette woman was unlocking the door and flipping the open sign. I asked for my box and she went into the back room for it. When she handed it to me I winced at how much it weighed. The box held four days of food—ostensibly enough to get me to Duncannon, Pennsylvania—146 miles south. I knew better. Despite my massive ingestion of calories at breakfast, I would need more for on the trail. Picking up some bars to bump my caloric total for each day, I piled them on the counter along with a pack cover. I was sick of everything I owned getting drenched.

"Rough one yesterday?" the woman asked, ringing me up.

"Yeah. Last straw. Time to get a pack cover. Say, what were those sirens for last night?"

"Oh, those were just to get the volunteers out to clear fallen trees off of the roads."

"Oh." Her answer was far less dramatic than the one I'd imagined.

Equipped with adequate supplies, a new poncho to replace the one shredded by the wind, and a new pack cover, I strode happily over to the Mount Minsi Trailhead.

"All right Rocksylvania, bring it on!"

The initial switchbacking climb up Mount Minsi and the subsequent ridge walk went smoothly. I took the short side trail to the Kirkridge shelter and utilized the faucet that runs to it from the retreat center, a stone's throw from the trail. There was no boil water advisory posted, but I ran it through my filter just to be safe. I powered on, thankful that—after the late start—the trail was decidedly less rocky than anticipated. The state's nickname among thru-hikers—Rocksylvania—had always seemed undeserved in my opinion, especially compared to New Hampshire and southern Maine. And, as I was discovering this time around, the rocks of Pennsylvania extended nearly to the northern border of New Jersey.

"Sorry, P," I said cheerfully. "You've got a bad rap."

It only took a few more hours of hiking for me find enough rocks to rescind my apology.

～

As I descended from the upper slopes of Blue Mountain into the deep gash of Lehigh Gap the following morning, I found myself scrambling again for the first time since New Hampshire. Instead of complaining, I laughed. Contorting and smearing my shoes against the boulders felt so natural and fun. My primary training for this hike had been climbing the highest peaks in Washington—off trail and semi-technical. The downclimbs felt like home to me. I paused to drink in the views of the Lehigh River far below and the swelling green ridges beyond—perpetual waves in an ancient granitic sea. The wind ruffled the hem of my skirt and I became acutely aware of the granular rock in my hands. I sensed the enormity of Blue Mountain hovering behind and beside me—a mere fragment of nature clinging to her southwestern ridge. I also perceived her sorrow at being raped by the zinc mines over a century ago. Yet she remained. The decades of revegetation work and superfund cleanup had been painstaking, but Blue had not been formed in a day and she hadn't been stripped in the same. The mountain was mighty and she would recover. She would someday reclaim her dignity. Reverently, I lowered myself down her rocks.

~

I turned left onto dirt Hawk Mountain Road and reached the Eckville shelter a quarter mile later. I smiled remembering what a respite it had been on my first hike: a fridge full of sodas, an enclosed shelter with bunks, a solar shower, potable water, and a friendly caretaker. At the water faucet I filled up, sat down, and plugged my phone in. I made an electrolyte drink and leaned my head against the refrigerator on the porch, staring up at the cloudless sky. My brand-new pack cover was still folded in the lid of my backpack, where it functioned as a sort of talisman. Not a drop had fallen since I bought it two days ago.

Despite the rocky footing throughout Pennsylvania, I'd been moving at a faster pace than before—covering well over forty miles a day since my first full day in the state. *And I'll do it again tonight.* The halfway point was imminent—pulling me southward. Each morning I woke in a fog of fatigue, sucked some caffeinated Trail Butter down, and got moving in less than fifteen minutes. I moved strong all day, refusing to stop until my legs were jelly—inevitably followed by a blissful collapse onto a messy pile of gear thrown around inside my tent, including my seldom-used sleeping bag. It had been so hot I hadn't needed to get in it for over four hundred miles. After a few spoonfuls of rehydrated beans mixed with coconut oil, I'd sleep for three to five hours. Repeated ad infinitum.

I pried myself up off the porch, unplugged my phone, and hoofed it back to the trail. Making my way up the old dirt road and into a watershed protection area, I started toward the popular promontories of the Pinnacle and Pulpit Rock. Twilight crept over me noiselessly, without a retinue of lightning or clouds; the mellow sunshine dissipated through the trees slowly until there was nothing left. I sauntered along, entranced by the rhythmic sound of my footfalls and clicks of my trekking poles. A small flash in my periphery made me turn. It came again.

"Fireflies," I whispered, as more began to glimmer.

Of all the things from the natural world I'd lost moving West, fireflies were one I truly missed. On many warm summer evenings I'd longed to hike like this, cocooned in velvet air and encircled by tiny green sparkles. I spun round, dancing with them. Their season had already ended when I'd started my hike, but this evening they were still illuminating the night. As dusk deepened and the air cooled, the fireflies faded away until I had only the stars for company.

~

I marched down Market Street as dusk graced the eastern mountaintops, intent on only one thing: picking up my box. One hundred and forty-seven miles of rocks had worn me down and I'd eaten my last snack on Peters Mountain hours ago. Moments later, the Doyle Hotel in downtown Duncannon came into view. I reached it and threw my pack on the bench outside.

After the harsh treatment at the AT Deli for accidentally bringing my pack in, I did not want a repeat. I walked into the bar and was immediately overcome by the tantalizing smell of burgers and fries.

"What can I do for you?" the man behind the bar asked.

"I have a box to pick up. Heather Anderson."

He looked me over. "Where's your pack?"

"I didn't know if I could bring it in so I left it outside."

"Go get it. Right now."

I was startled by his serious tone and scampered back outside to pick it up. It was not tampered with, but as I glanced around, I realized Duncannon was a bit rough around the edges—not an ideal location to leave a pack unattended. Back inside, I reached the counter as the man was returning from the back with my box.

"Thank you," I said.

"You staying the night?"

I turned to look at the man drinking beer beside me who'd asked the question.

"Um, no."

"I'm a trail angel. Bob. I'm happy to pay for your room. You look like you need a rest."

"Oh, thank you," I said, flustered. The man behind the bar held out the clipboard for me to sign for my box. "But no."

Even though I declined firmly, the truth was I very much wanted to stay. I wanted to stay for three days, like I did in 2003. I wanted to sleep in a bed, no matter how worn out. I wanted a shower and three cheeseburgers and umpteen french fries doused in ketchup. I glanced behind the bar at the specials sign. Instead of a list of menu items it said, "Congratulations Matt Kirk Sub-60 days." The words were like a slap across the face, reminding me why I was on the Appalachian Trail this summer. I was here to put 100 percent into every day and find my best. Not stop at nightfall and give in to the lure of burgers and a shower.

"Did you want some food?" the bartender asked.

I brought my eyes back to him, realizing he and Bob had both been staring at me for an unknown amount of time.

"Oh. No. No, thank you. I need to put in a few more miles tonight."

He turned away and Bob returned to his beer. I dumped the resupply into my pack without sorting it.

Back on the street, I followed roads to the edge of town and across Sherman Creek at its confluence with the umber waters of the capacious Susquehanna River. Darkness engulfed the river valley as I followed the trail uphill, climbing toward the Hawk Rock Overlook and beyond to Cove Mountain shelter. I'd been dreading this section for days. Two decades prior a couple had been brutally murdered at the Cove Mountain shelter. The absolute last place I wanted to be hiking at eventide was near a bygone murder scene. Yet, the sign at the Doyle had served as a kick in the pants strong enough to get me to face my irrational fears.

The thousand-foot climb was arduous, made more difficult by my mental state. There were no fireflies to distract and accompany me. Cove Mountain brooded in the gloom. Whether it was my own mind or the mountain herself I did not know, but I felt an uneasy sense of what had happened there permeating the shadows. I finally made camp forty miles from where I'd awakened.

It was a fitful sleep. When my alarm sounded at 4 a.m., I didn't even eat. I simply threw everything into my pack and headed out into the fog. My lights reflected off of the water vapor, adding to the eeriness of the place. I knew it was irrational to be frightened, but I was. A few tears snuck out and I wiped them away angrily.

"Stop it. There's nothing to be afraid of," I said loudly. "The chronic sleep deprivation is catching up with you. Don't be a scaredy-cat."

I stumbled along the short, jabbing rocks jutting from the ground until I finally broke out of the trees. The fog swirled and cavorted as I passed through a gas pipeline clearing, teasing me with phantasms. I hastened back into the trees, and the trail began to descend steeply. After crossing a stream on a wooden footbridge, I emerged into a dewy field. There the sunrise filtered through swirls of mist, causing the world to gleam a lustrous mother-of-pearl. I exhaled with relief, watching my breath dissipate slowly.

I set my pack on the ground and put away my headlamp. From here I would wind through fields and over a ridge before descending to cross the prodigious Cumberland Valley. For over twenty miles the terrain would be gradual and decidedly non-rocky. I pulled out enough food to quell my roaring stomach and took off.

There was no need to ration as I made my way toward Boiling Springs—anything I ate in excess could be replenished at the gas station there. The sun burned through the fog, revealing an idyllic landscape of lush, green pastures and quaint farmsteads. I cruised along at over three miles per hour for what felt like the first time in my life. As I drew closer to Boiling Springs, I passed more homes as well as joggers, cyclists, and dog walkers enjoying the greenway that was the AT corridor. They nodded acknowledgement, smiled, or waved.

I was over one thousand miles deep into this endeavor and no one asked if I was a day hiker anymore. Despite my small backpack, I knew I looked like someone who had been *through something*: the slightly desperate-looking eyes that were hungry for miles as well as meals. My chest had flattened, and my hip belt now sagged uselessly. Every ounce of fat had melted off of my legs, revealing the muscles of steel—etched by miles, mountains, and propulsion—that lay beneath. The hemline of my dress was tattered. I was absolutely filthy and I stank. Yet as I forged my way along the wide footpath, my stride was all business. Even that morning I'd covered the uneven terrain without difficulty. *No one can think I am anything but what I am: a southbounder.*

I reached the Lakeside Food Mart at midday and emptied their entire row of Reese's Pieces. Additionally, I bought a cold Coke and a bag of salt-and-vinegar chips. At the Appalachian Trail Conservancy's field office—right on trail—I plugged my phone in and filled my water. Settling in at the picnic table in front of the small building, I devoured my fill of calories, washing them down with soda. I'd managed to cover twenty-two miles by noon. There wasn't a single storm cloud in sight. After half an hour, my phone 80 percent full, I rousted myself from my break. Despite everything I'd eaten, my pack was still heavy.

I probably didn't need ten packages of Reese's, I thought ruefully.

It was about one hundred trail miles from Boiling Springs to the main ATC office in Harpers Ferry. Between the two locations lay the trail's halfway point in southern Pennsylvania—about a day's journey for me. If I kept my miles up, I would be at Harpers in two days.

I'm going to complete half the trail in twenty-nine days, I realized. Not on pace to break the record—tie it if I'm lucky. But I'm doing my best. That's all that matters.

The rest of the Cumberland Valley flew by in a blur of road crossings and cow pastures. The thought that I was well off from my initial ideal pace, as well as the pace needed to set the self-supported record, lingered in the back of my mind. I was well ahead of the women's self-supported time, which was over twenty days slower than the men's, but I'd come to set an overall record. The disappointment threatened to overthrow the full-belly high I'd been riding along the easy trail.

"You were barely hanging on to Scott's record at the halfway point of the PCT too, Anish."

I hadn't thought of it earlier, but as soon as the words were out of my mouth, free to soar over the rolling ridges of the East, I felt lighter. My confidence from that morning returned. I was going to keep doing my best. I was going to see it through. No matter what, I was not relenting until I reached Springer Mountain, Georgia—1,100 miles away.

~

Hours later, I squinted in the faint twilight as I tried to follow white-blazed posts through Pine Grove Furnace State Park. I set my pack down at the fountain outside the restrooms and started to fill my water bladder. I was bone-tired, but I still had another five miles to reach fifty for the day. *If I can't do fifty miles across the Cumberland, I'm never going to be able to do fifty on this trail.*

"The park is closed! What are you doing?"

I nearly dropped my water bladder at the man's voice. I spun around to see a security guard running across the lawn at me.

"I was just getting water."

He slowed at the sight of me standing there with a half-full bladder in my hands.

"The park closes at dark," he repeated, coming to a stop ten feet away.

"Oh, I didn't know the Appalachian Trail ever closed. I'm just hiking through. I needed water." I raised my bladder.

The guard made a noncommittal noise. I wasn't sure he knew whether the trail was open or not. I didn't know either, but I did know the park had a campground—I hadn't imagined I couldn't hike through at dusk.

"Well, just don't stop again."

"Don't worry. I want to get to the next shelter more than you want me to."

The corners of his mouth twitched a bit and he nodded. I went back to filling my bladder and he went back to his car. He sat there until I resumed following the white blazes south. A half mile later I reached the entrance road to the park and began climbing away from civilization. By the time I reached the former AT midpoint—marked with an elaborate timber structure—I was dragging. A short distance later I heard people laughing and talking at the Toms Run shelter. For some reason I hadn't anticipated it being full of people. The fitful night of sleep on top of the high mileage days through Connecticut, Massachusetts, New York, New Jersey, and Pennsylvania were beginning to overwhelm my body and brain. I'd planned to camp here, but the noise at the shelter drove me to continue. Not too much farther along the trail I found a place to camp.

After throwing my tent up haphazardly, I lay down thinking yet again about quitting. *Why continue when you're barely holding on?* Although I had finally hiked fifty miles, I was still dissatisfied that it was anomalous, rather than the norm. I toyed with the cheetah necklace that hung around my neck. "Fastest land mammal," my boyfriend had said when he gave it to me before I boarded the plane.

I'd thanked him, but at the time—and now—I thought, *I am not fast.* Relentless. Stubborn. Able to endure, yes, but not truly fast. Not truly athletic. *It is my mind that is forcing my body forward. Not my body being able.*

"I've never wrestled with the 'Q word' as much as I have on this hike," I said quietly, aloud.

Despite my frequent moments of resolve, I'd wanted to quit every day. Yet, deep inside, I knew there was an answer that I would find—I simply had to keep doing my best until I found it. I wondered if it was my drive that had formed the very walls I now needed to topple to find the answer. I knew that if it was, I was the only one capable of doing so—by pushing myself toward the physical brink, my limit, wherever it lay.

I stirred water into that day's ration of dehydrated refried beans and sealed it shut. Then I lay back down on my side and put the beans down at nose level. I stared as it rehydrated, barely able to keep my eyes open. Every day I battled with self-doubt in a way I hadn't on the PCT. There I'd been too caught up in what was happening *to* me. It was only now that I began to realize I was not simply in a passive role, but was myself the acting force. I mushed the beans, massaging the water through the thickening paste.

"There is no question I'm forging this journey," I mused. "I'm seeking rather than being carried along by a tidal wave. I felt inevitability as I crossed from Oregon to Washington, believing fate would carry me to Canada. But here, I'm closing in on halfway and there is absolutely no gliding."

Every step was an agreement with myself to do my best, to leave nothing in reserve except the bare minimum I needed for the next day. I opened the bag and started eating my dinner.

I was finding that in the years since I'd become Anish out here, the trail hadn't changed much. It was still steep and unforgiving, laden with rocks and roots and mud. The views were usually obscured by trees and vegetation. I still worked impossibly hard for every summit. Even finishing a hike this grueling was an accomplishment. Could I possibly feel any prouder standing on Springer in 2015 than I had standing on Katahdin in 2003? *I doubt it.*

On a thru-hike with an attrition rate of over 50 percent, I wasn't sure what had made a two-hundred-pound girl from the flatlands who'd barely even camped overnight believe she could traverse the Appalachian Mountains from Georgia to Maine. *What makes me think I can set a record out here now?* I knew deep down I held tightly to the belief I was destined to do something different with my life. That belief was also rooted in sheer stubbornness. *I may not be the fastest, like the cheetah I wear close to my heart, but I am definitely the most determined.*

I finished eating, lay back down, and clicked my headlamp off. When I'd stood on Springer Mountain in May of 2003, I was untested and blissfully ignorant. I knew one thing and one thing only: come hell or high water, I was walking every step to Maine. Now I was going back there, this time with twenty thousand miles of hiking under my feet and enough experience and knowledge to know I was in over my head. I was also aware that no matter the cost, I wanted to make it to Springer Mountain. I was no longer an overweight flatlander without a clue: I was a cheetah in training.

~

I reached the current Appalachian Trail midpoint at sunrise—the macabre-named Dead Womans Hollow Road. I paused to look at the small laminated sign hanging on the tree, congratulating hikers on their achievement. With trail work changing the AT's mileage every year, the mobile laminated sign was a significantly better option than the enormous pole I'd passed the night before. *Although the wooden marker makes for better photos.* I thought about my halfway point on the PCT. I thought about what it had taken to get here. I thought—inevitably—about how much farther I had to go.

It takes a certain level of insanity to seek a record on a two-thousand-mile-long trail. To dedicate oneself to physical drain and psychological intensity for such a prolonged distance. The focus required for well over a month was more than was needed for pretty much any other athletic endeavor. Yet here I was again for the second time in three years. Perhaps I *was* insane. I shrugged the thought off. I'd learned to accept myself and my desire to hike on the lonely miles along the PCT. Now I was here because it felt like the right thing to do—the only thing.

I walked into Maryland as evening drew nigh, barely pausing at the Mason-Dixon Line sign. I wanted to reach Harpers Ferry by the thirty-day mark. Despite all of the setbacks I still believed I could hike the AT in sixty days, the same amount of time it had taken me to complete the Pacific Crest Trail, which was over four hundred miles longer. I'd reached the halfway point of the PCT on day thirty-two, so I was already ahead of that pace.

Perhaps I can tie Matt's fifty-eight-day record after all, I thought. If I can just stay focused and strong . . . and not have any more setbacks.

By ten—hiking by headlamp once again—I was approaching forty-five miles for the day. I came to the turnoff for the Ensign Cowall shelter and debated taking the side trail a tenth of a mile to get water. The guidebook indicated it would be a seep, but the miles ahead were dry and I needed to sleep soon. On faith, I took off my pack, pulled out my baggie of dehydrated refried beans, and poured the last of my water into it. I headed down the side trail, past the shelter and the privy, to the spring—thankful to find it flowing. After gathering water from the trickling source, I crept back past the sleeping hikers inside the lean-to, and glanced at the decrepit picnic table in front. I remembered sitting there in 2003 with several others, gorging on pizza and breadsticks we'd had delivered to the highway crossing not far to the south. I reached my pack and picked up the now-hydrated beans. Sitting on a rock, I bit off the corner of the baggie and squeezed some into my mouth. While eating, I filtered my water into my bottle and put my pack back on.

As I left rocky footing for trail around a pasture, I gazed up at the sky. Entranced by the twinkling stars, I moved south toward Springer, still sucking my dinner from the corner of the bag.

"I really wonder sometimes, how exactly I became this woman," I said to the night.

A woman who slept in the woods, ate to move, drank from wild waters, and crushed miles to clear her soul. A woman covered in dirt, with unshaven legs, and an authentic smile. A woman who was both feral and content. I ascended yet another rocky ridge bounded by trees forming a thin veil between civilization and wilderness. In the daytime the nearby cities were hard to see through the leafy screen, but at night the lights of Fredericksburg and Hagerstown glimmered in consort with the ancient stars aloft. As long as I remained here, shrouded from that world, I was blissful. Those stars had borne witness to my formation and would far surpass my brief lifetime, just like the rocks beneath my tired feet. I could be myself before them. Nakedness in their presence never made me feel vulnerable. Yet the city lights, the society I'd been born into, always would, no matter how many layers I wore.

"Heather, you need to let people in. Those who care about you. Stop pushing everyone away."

Words from 2003, when I was volunteering at humanitarian organizations in Washington, DC, came to me, unbidden and still biting.

"I don't see what this has to do with my performance evaluation," I said, staring at the leader of the university trip, defying her to continue. I could earn a credit for participation and a paper—and I'd done both.

She relented. "You attended every volunteer opportunity and did an excellent job performing what was asked of you."

I walked away with my signed paperwork—angry. I'd spent my entire spring break with a group of people from my university that I didn't know, trying to do something good. Instead I was being told that I was doing something wrong. That I was wrong. That there was something wrong with me. It seemed that every day of my life I'd been told the same thing. I had never fit in. I'd never been the right size or shape. I was too awkward and shy. I wasn't athletic. I just couldn't get it right. There was no denying the fact that I was wrong. A failure at everything outside of academics.

I went into the bunk room and sat by the window. Cold rain sputtered from the sky. On the street I could see the people from my group laughing and talking, walking back from wherever they had gone for lunch. I didn't even remember when I'd last eaten. I knew no one understood why I wouldn't go out with them.

I was leaving for the Appalachian Trail in two months. Whatever I managed to save from my part-time jobs between now and then was all I would have to hike on. Keeping that perspective helped me to skip meals and ignore the temptation to spend money. Graduating debt-free had been a goal of mine even before the AT, but once I decided to hike, it became imperative.

I had no idea what the trail would actually be like, but no matter, it was going to be better than my college life. Studying day and night to keep up my GPA in order to retain my scholarships and grants. Packing my academic schedule each semester, working multiple part-time jobs. I had realized too late that my father had been right to encourage me to take the scholarship to MSU rather than a private university in another state.

The noise of the rest of the group coming up the hostel stairs urged me away from the window. I crawled into my bunk and picked up my book: John Muir's A Thousand-Mile Walk to the Gulf. *Then again, if I had gone to MSU, would I be here right now, reading the words of a Scottish conservationist and planning to walk across the country? Would I know what it was like to work incredibly hard and sleep very little and sacrifice so much to have both a college degree and the trail? I doubted it.*

~

My misfiture into the human world happened long before I'd ever started walking long distances. Perhaps I'd been born that way, but my many miles on trail had made me more comfortable in nature than anywhere else. More comfortable in the presence of wild animals and trees than with people.

I had believed the people who'd told me there was something wrong with me. I'd taken their words and flagellated myself with them over and over, every time I felt low or vulnerable. Every time I was embarrassed at how badly I fit into my culture, I'd rejected my own essential self. I was not certain how I'd lost my connection to the world I'd been born into, but I now knew that there was nothing wrong with me and I would never regret trading it for kinship with stardust and bedrock.

~

The Appalachian Trail Conservancy Headquarters was a quarter mile off the AT. I followed a blue-blazed trail leading into the outskirts of Harpers Ferry, West Virginia. My nearly empty pack swung back and forth merrily as I took the steps up two at a time. I jogged down sidewalks interspersed with cobblestones to the white stone building I remembered fondly. My heart soared at the sight of the spiritual halfway point of the trail. I'd covered the remainder of Maryland and was now well into the small slice of West Virginia the AT crossed. I'd sleep in Virginia that night, but first I needed to get my box.

"New shoes!" I couldn't help but squeal with joy at the sight of new shoes and socks in the box when I opened it.

I pulled them out and set them down beside me. The hiker lounge the AT Conservancy provided was comfortable, and I couldn't have been happier to spend two dollars on four Cokes from their hiker fridge. I pulled out the pouch of Indian food in my box and devoured it.

I stepped outside for my requisite thru-hiker picture and wrote my info on a piece of paper for their records.

"Anish. 8/1 start at Katahdin. 9/1 Harpers Ferry. Southbound."

I stared at it. My loping handwriting was bigger and more rampant than normal, having not written a single word since the note I'd left Steve and Sue at the Hiker Hut. I'd gone 1,166 miles in thirty days. Something about putting it there in print made the endeavor more real. From there south, I knew one thing: I had to remain all in.

I finished my fourth soda and dressed my dirty feet in new shoes and socks. After thanking the friendly staff, I headed back to the trail. I had miles to go before I could sleep.

VIRGINIA BLUES

THROUGH THE TREES, I watched sunset gild the valleys and forests to the west as I traveled the boundary line separating West Virginia and Virginia. The Appalachian Trail was truly a crest trail—more so even than the PCT—frequently weaving along the top of the Eastern Continental Divide. I passed the turnoff to the ATC's trail crew cabin—the Blackburn Trail Center—as a man descending from a spur trail pointed behind him at the top of the ridge.

"Great view of the sunset from up there."

I nodded. "Thanks."

He paused, obviously anticipating that I would turn up the side trail before heading down to the trail center campground. Instead, I kept moving south. I'd already been watching the sun's inexorable transit toward its daily denouement for the last twenty minutes. Witnessing the finale from an outcrop off trail would simply be a bonus.

"And I don't need bonus miles," I mumbled, pulling my headlamp out of the pocket of my grimy dress.

I used to be terrified of the dark, before I'd forced myself to face that fear two years ago on the PCT. Now, night-hiking felt comfortable. Each day I slid into it as I would into slippers after a long run and a hot shower. Each day the earth sank into shadow without hesitation, so why shouldn't I? I smiled at the changes in myself. I'd learned courage. And from that courage had come confidence. And from that confidence had grown acceptance of all circumstances.

Virginia contained more of the AT than any other state—over 500 miles. I planned to cover those miles in ten days, just as I'd done on Oregon's 455 miles of the PCT where I'd also averaged 50 miles per day. I hoped I could dig deep enough to find that strength again. At least this time I was better nourished.

"If I ever get off the rocks," I growled, tripping over a jagged edge sticking straight up in the middle of the trail. "Rockslyvania starts in Jersey and ends in Virginia, apparently."

I sighed. The AT was simply an arduous trail. The rocks were omnipresent, but the level of difficulty they presented did ebb and flow. I knew at some point Virginia would give way to verdant pastoral landscapes and rolling hills with better tread. Much like Vermont. *But not tonight.*

Near midnight I found an area with fewer rocks and threw my tent on the ground. A movement caught my eye and I jerked my light in its direction. A long black spider the size of a tarantula darted for cover under the tent.

"Oh no you don't!" I screamed at it and flung the tent aside.

Using my trekking pole, I prodded at the spider until it scurried into some rocks. I rapidly examined the underside of my tent for additional arachnids and set it up in haste. In the process, another spider of the same dimensions ran into the circle of headlamp light. I sent it flying with my trekking pole and then crawled inside my tent—zipping it closed against any intruder. I shuddered involuntarily before thoroughly examining myself and my gear for hitchhikers.

Satisfied I was alone in my shelter, I prepared for bed. All the while, I could see two enormous spiders patrolling the perimeter of my camp through the tent's mesh panels. I shuddered again and verified that there were no holes in my tent.

"God, I hate spiders," I muttered. *Hate is an understatement, Anish. You're phobic of spiders. Perhaps now that you've conquered the night, you can conquer arachnids?*

Sighing, I lay down and clicked off my headlamp.

~

I topped the last hill of the infamous Roller Coaster and turned around.

"More appropriately called the rocky coaster," I grumbled.

Despite the series of short, steep, rocky climbs and descents over the prior fourteen miles—garnering the stretch its nickname—I'd still managed to get twenty miles in by one in the afternoon. The exertion needed to plow uphill and downhill had been aided in the final miles by music blaring in my ears. Now, solidly in the state of Virginia and no longer paralleling the border, I was out of the worst of the rocks. I did a little dance to celebrate before turning the music off and heading south toward Ashby Gap. A few miles prior I'd found "1,000" spelled out in stones across the trail. It had taken me a few moments to process the enormity of its meaning. Placed there by northbounders, it meant I only had one thousand miles left.

"Only," I snorted.

I thought about my camp at the one-thousand-mile mark in the Sierra, north of Dorothy Lake Pass. How I'd cried myself to sleep, uncertain if I could possibly give more than I'd already given. How I'd felt defeated by the thousand miles of desert and altitude—unable to comprehend a similar effort for 1,600 more. Yet, I had. One footstep, one mile, one day at a time. Now, here I was, on the opposite side of the equation—and the country—over 1,200 miles in and counting down.

Thrilled to have the rockiest part of the mid-Atlantic behind me, I let myself melt into the soft sounds of the woods. Even a busy highway crossing didn't dispel the serenity I felt. I climbed up from the thoroughfare on well-graded trail into Sky Meadows State Park. White-blazed posts sprouted in a line across expansive grasslands where I could breathe deeply of the heavens above. A nemophilist, I loved dwelling in the womb of the forest. Yet, these moments allowed me to unfurl and blossom upward toward the unobstructed sky.

Down the other side of the uplands, I refilled my water from the gushing spring at the Manassas Gap shelter. Hours later, shadows deepened as I followed stone remnants of Mosby's line: now nearly invisible, this was once part of a stalwart boundary of the Confederate army. I moved through the darkening forest, aware that some of the soldiers still lingered. Mist rose from the ground and capered in and out of my headlamp's beam. Rustling in nearby leaves pricked the hairs on my neck and arms as I resolutely continued.

"I'm not stopping until I get to Shenandoah."

I crossed deserted Route 522, descended steeply to cross the creek over a bridge, and followed the muddy trail as it skimmed past people's homes. Wafting through the windows were the sounds of clamoring televisions and smells from enticing dinners. A cloud of droplets hovered over the trail, glistening with the chemicals of modern life. I held my breath as I cleaved a path through the dryer exhaust, bathing in the moist heat. The smell of fabric softener clung to me as I passed back into the trees.

It was nearly 2,000 vertical feet up to Shenandoah National Park, further to the aptly named Skyline Drive that I would dance with for a hundred miles across the park. My feet slowed to a shuffle as I climbed, the day's final three miles dragging into the late hours. At midnight I found myself free of switchbacks and standing at a kiosk. I scanned the instructions for registering to backpack through the park. Crawling into the forest, I set up my tent amid the rocks just outside the park boundary. Less than four hours after I closed my eyes, I entered the park.

~

Perhaps the most appreciated part about the Appalachian Trail through Shenandoah National Park, at least among thru-hikers, is that it travels within a short distance of the main park highway—Skyline Drive—the entire way. A variety of roadside pullouts are therefore easy for hikers to access—opportunities for trash cans, food, showers, and laundry make the trail through the park a decidedly cushy experience. Unless, of course, you are trying to hike the trail in less than sixty days.

I arrived at the Loft Mountain Camp Store—just a few yards off the trail—at two in the afternoon. The showers were closed, but I plugged my phone into the outlet in the breezeway and went inside the store. My next resupply would be at the twenty-four-hour Kroger supermarket in Daleville on the I-80 interchange—162 miles south.

"I'll be there in three days," I told myself as I carried my basket around the small store.

In 2013, I'd determinedly covered fifty miles per day across Oregon. I'd also been starving to the point of passing out, I reminded myself. The trail there was well graded—three miles per hour had been easy to maintain for hours on end, even when I was depleted. Virginia would be another story altogether. Yet, whether my miscalculations were due to rampant optimism or sleep deprivation compromising my math skills, I would later regret my three-day resupply plan.

I left Loft Mountain fueled by ice cream and coffee. Despite the caloric perk, I felt strained, mentally and physically. *Will I fall apart again like I did in Oregon?* Already I was barely managing forty-eight miles a day in Virginia and it was taking me until midnight. My hold on Matt's time was tenuous. *How many more days can I go with only four hours of sleep?* I kicked at leaves as I hiked, lost in thought.

A once familiar sound—one I'd nearly forgotten—snapped me out of it. I glanced up to see dark clouds coalescing. Lightning arced across them. I felt my mood sink even lower. *At least I get to use my new pack cover.* I donned my poncho, secured the pack cover, and resigned myself to several wet hours of hiking.

~

I'd envisioned September bringing comfortable, sunny days and crisp nights. Instead, it brought empty trails—even in a national park—oppressive humidity, and unwavering summer heat. Abandoned graves and homesteads bore silent testimony that someone had once been here, but I saw no one now except near road crossings. The springs mentioned in the guides were either tiny pools, or nonexistent. All day long, I cleared spiderwebs spanning the trail with my body, and sometimes my face. Each time I shrieked, swatting the sticky filigree from my sweaty skin and frantically flicking the spiders away. It seemed as though I stopped more than I walked in some sections, flinging yellow orb weavers off of myself in a panic.

Thunder rolled and I plopped down at the picnic table under the covered porch of the palatial Paul Wolfe shelter. I did not want to climb up from the hollow where it was located into the storm hurling both rain and lightning. Fed up with climbing into storms, I was thankful that I'd only had to deal with a few while I traversed the high terrain of Shenandoah. Now that I was out of the park, there were more dips in the terrain where I could hide from the weather.

"I hate spiders," I said aloud, wiping a cobweb off of my shin, pulling my knees to my chest, and setting my chin on them. "I can't take it anymore. I really just can't. I can't stand being covered in spiders and webs all the time."

The pounding of the rain on the roof was deafening. Maybe the deluge would knock down any webs lying in wait across the trail. I idly thought about quitting. *I'd never have to walk through a spiderweb again.* I pulled out a bar and chewed on it while investigating the remaining contents of my food bag.

"I should have bought more. A lot more."

In truth, it had been hard to scrounge up enough gluten-free, lightweight food for three days at the Loft Mountain Camp Store—not to mention how expensive it'd been. I'd spent one hundred dollars on three days of food at 3,000 calories per day. My average was ten to twelve dollars a day.

And I should be eating 3,500 a day now.

The box in Harpers Ferry had had that much, and so did my box ahead in Bland. I'd been so preoccupied with getting supplies and getting back on the trail that I'd failed to do either task well. I'd underbought and I'd tripped in my haste to leave the store, banging my knee on a rock. I probed it gently with my chin—finding it still tender and slightly swollen. It was going to take me almost five full days to get from Loft Mountain to Daleville, not three.

"I'm not going to make it."

The rain was tapering off and—though the storm was still booming—I knew if I sat there any longer I would regret it after nightfall. Fatigue always set in after sixteen hours of wakefulness, but it often took an additional hour or two to reach exhaustion. I still wasn't hitting fifty miles—consistently falling one or two miles short every day—but I was doing all I could do. The ephemeral best was breaking me and carrying me south at the same time. But my lack of food meant I needed to maximize my mileage each day, otherwise I might have nothing to eat for the last thirty miles.

"I need twenty-three more miles today—spiders and storms be damned," I said resolutely.

After all, you can't quit because of spiders, I finished in my head.

The rain did not stop, although the thunder did. I was happy to find that the rain gods had seen fit to "wash the spider out" after all, which put me in higher spirits. Reaching the turnoff to Maupin shelter at dusk, I hurried down to get water only to find that the spring behind it was nonexistent. However, a puddle of rainwater had collected in the depression. I hurried to scoop it into my bladder.

"You're not staying?" a woman in the shelter asked as I walked back.

"No, gotta do a few more miles tonight."

"Be safe. It's going to be dark soon."

I nodded to her and the others set up inside the dark three-sided building and headed back up the blue-blazed trail to the AT. On the way, I passed four people heading toward the shelter. They looked at me with confusion—I was hiking away from the shelter at seven in the evening after all—but I didn't pause to engage. I was sapped from the miles, lack of sleep, lack of calories, and from constantly flirting with dehydration.

"I'm literally drinking from a puddle," I said. I shook my head at myself, but I was too thirsty to really care where my water was from. *At least the rain stopped.*

The mountainous mass of Three Ridges towered above me, hidden by the dripping forest and growing darkness.

"Three miles and 3,000 feet." I closed the elevation profile on the Guthook app.

I tried not to think about it. I tried not to think about the four additional miles down the other side. I most definitely tried not to think about the ascent of The Priest—nearly 4,000 feet over five miles—waiting for me on the far side of the river tomorrow morning. I tried to simply think about putting my feet down one in front of the other, methodically making my way forward. My pace slowed after I passed over the nondescript subsummit of Bee Mountain. Despite the exertion, I seemed to be no closer to the top of Three Ridges, and thus no closer to sleep. I felt a slight weave creep into my walk. My blinks grew longer and longer. *I'll just camp at the top.* The thought of stopping at the top of the mountain, after forty-four miles, comforted me. I was nearing my limit already. *No need to push farther. You've done your best today.* I paused to pull out a commercially dehydrated meal and poured some water into it. I swished the liquid around, sealed it, and tucked it into the pocket of my pack. It usually took three hours to fully rehydrate without boiling water, but in an hour it would at least be edible. I resumed my upward trajectory.

A darting movement on the trail brought my wandering mind back to the present. I quickly halted—my primitive instincts taking control of my legs while my dulled mind lagged in identifying the sinuous shape moving toward me. Its pinkish coloration, illumined by the beam of my headlamp, was beautiful, like cotton candy clouds at sunset.

The snake arrested its forward progress six inches from my feet. I stared at it—uncomprehending—as its tongue darted in and out, searching to understand the obstruction. Two solo travelers had arrived at a nighttime impasse.

It's got a viper head, but it's not rattling. I struggled to make sense of the sensory input. *Where are the rattles? Why isn't it rattling? I don't understand. Why isn't it rattling?*

As if an electric shock had zapped us simultaneously, we danced away from each other. I leaped rightward, screaming, "Copperhead!" The snake lunged the opposite way, darting for cover beneath the leaf litter. I landed farther up trail and spun around, scanning the ground for the copperhead. I half expected it to be there, chasing me. Instead, I saw nothing and heard only a slight rustle of leaves down the hill, belying the serpent's presence. Backing up the trail a few feet, I whirled around and ascended at a rapid clip, riding the wave of adrenaline flooding my veins. The brush with a venomous snake had roused me from my lassitude and I powered through the remaining mile to the summit.

To my absolute frustration, every potential campsite was inhabited by a tent. I felt tears well up as a gentle breeze wafted through the trees. *It's almost midnight and there's no place to camp.* The surge of energy from the copperhead encounter drained out of me and, in its void, came another wave—crushing weariness. I began to descend Three Ridges—resigned to walking until I found a campsite somewhere in the four-mile, 3,000-foot descent. *Surely there has to be another spot.*

The trail began to switchback in earnest. *Down, down, down. . . .* I kept my eyes glued to the ground for more snakes. I felt my mind disconnect again, even as I tried hard to keep it focused. I grasped at the end of the frayed wire. I would not let it go as I had on the John Muir Trail.

"I'm Anish. I'm on the AT. I'm trying to set the record," I whispered to myself in a string of reassurances that I still knew who and where I was.

The temperature lowered until it was practically pleasant. I had a vague realization it was the Saturday of Labor Day weekend. Suddenly the droves camped at Maupin and Three Ridges made sense. I'd lost the concept of time somewhere in the mud of the AT. I not only had no idea where I was in relation to the record, I didn't even know the day of the week or month unless I checked on my phone. Even the hours were indiscernible; time was like the wall clock I'd had as a teenager, where the numerals lay in a jumbled pile at the bottom even though the hands kept time. I existed there—and there alone—in that messy heap of disordered integers.

The trail zigzagged endlessly. I checked my phone repeatedly. The campsite listed at the bottom never drew any closer. Each minute seemed to last an hour with my glacial pace. The trail grew rockier—more than it had been in over a hundred miles. Worst of all, there was nowhere to camp in the steep terrain. My legs shook with fatigue and lack of calories. Again, I rebuked myself for miscalculating my last resupply.

"Rationing is a terrible thing," I growled to myself. "Why are you so bad at math? Can't you do anything right?"

The fall happened so fast I had no time to react. I tripped on a rock and my overwrought body simply couldn't catch me. One second I was walking and the next I was lying in a talus-laden section of trail: my body draped over and around large rocks, arms and legs turned outward at unnatural angles. My right cheek lay flat against a chunk of cool granite. Vegetable beef stew slowly oozed out of my rehydrating meal into my hair and down the side of my face where it dripped off my chin and onto the ground.

I lay there, vaguely surprised to find myself prone. The stew continued its slow progress as I settled into an awareness of my body's new position in relation to the earth. One hand still grasped a trekking pole. The other hand did not. My right arm was outstretched overhead. The left was tucked beneath my body—shoulder rolled under me. My left leg was suspended by a small boulder under my hip—my shin dangled inward, flexing from the knee joint. My right foot was twisted, toes anchored beneath a chunk of talus. Its corresponding knee hovered in a pocket of open space between sharp edged stones. The ribs above my breasts ached. I wasn't sure if I was injured. I was simply grateful to be lying down.

"I just want to sleep," I whispered.

I thought about getting up. Yet, despite being heaped at odd angles on hard surfaces, I yearned to stay put. I considered leaving my eyes closed and letting myself enter unconsciousness. *I don't need a campsite. I can sleep here.* After a few moments of thinking along those lines, I began to feel twinges of pain percolating through the shock of the fall and the miasma of exhaustion.

"Damn. Dammit."

I leaned all my weight forward onto my face and right hand—the only leverage I had against the decline. Awkwardly, I unfurled my left shoulder and freed my hand to steady myself as I staggered to a standing position. Leaning on the remaining trekking pole, gasping for air, I realized how much my ribs and lungs ached. So did my right ankle and both knees—which oozed blood, shining crimson in the dazzle of my headlamp. I panned my light around slowly until I spotted the lost pole five feet away, vaguely remembering the sensation of it being flung from my hand as I fell. I hobbled over and picked it up—relieved to see it wasn't broken—then made my way carefully across the rocks and onto dirt trail again. Leaning heavily on the poles, I inched down the trail, uncertain whether or not I was truly hurt. Great shaking sobs roiled out of me, the kind that come when you have reached literal or figurative rock bottom—in this case, both.

"Dammit. I can't do this!" I cried, my shock giving way to anger. "I just can't do this anymore."

The stiffness in my body relented slightly as I forced it to move.

"This is it. I am done for real this time. I just can't do this anymore. I need more food and more sleep. I need less humidity, less lightning, less spiders, and less rocks. I am at the end of my rope."

I sob-screamed to God, the universe, the darkness around me—anything that would listen.

"If you want me to do this, something has to give!"

It wasn't an ultimatum, but a statement of fact. I knew I could only deal with so much hardship and sleep deprivation before I broke. I'd reached that point. Hot tears poured out of my eyes, borne from equal parts overwhelming frustration and the pain of the fall. Yet anger fueled me forward as I hobbled faster, willing my body to function properly.

"I did this because I thought it was a calling!" I stopped in the trail, gasping for breath as I battled with whether I needed to cry or to yell more urgently. "I can't do this alone."

I looked up at the handful of stars glimmering through the trees. My yelling had silenced the nocturnal sounds of the Appalachian forest. I reached up and wiped beef stew off of my face and shoulder strap—then I smeared it on the bark of a tree. The ludicrousness of my position—bruised, bleeding, crying, and covered in stew while standing in the middle of the Appalachian Trail after midnight screaming at God like Job—was not lost on me. My sobs lessened and I found I could finally breathe evenly, though a trickle of tears continued.

A soft familiar voice, the one that had always driven me forward, whispered inside my mind: *"When you look back, tonight will be a turning point."*

I trudged onward. No matter my demands, afflictions, or assuaging answers, I still had to find a place to sleep.

By the time I found a campsite near Harpers Creek it was well after one in the morning. Zombie-like, I set my tent up by rote. Then I splashed creek water on my face, arm, and pack to clean off my dinner before crawling into my sleeping bag without changing clothes or socks. I managed to spoon what was left of the stew into my mouth before lying back and checking my watch: 2 a.m.

~

I had to swim through a deep ocean of sleep chemicals to reach the alarm when it sounded two hours later. I could barely comprehend the noise. My limbs were still immobilized and my eyelids were too heavy to open, weighed down by yesterday's twenty-one hours of continuous movement. When at last I managed to grasp my watch, my fingers fumbled with the buttons. I wasn't sure any time had passed while I'd been unconscious. I felt the same as when I'd fallen asleep—possibly more exhausted. The opacity of night was still thick outside my tent; the creek was still merrily burbling nearby. It was hard to believe my watch.

I thought about the trail ahead. It was a short walk to the road. Then up one of the hardest climbs in all of Virginia—a mountain called The Priest. *Or, I could stop now. I could sleep for as long as I wanted, walk to the road, and get a ride. A ride to anywhere with a motel and food. Where I could sleep some more. For days if I wanted.*

"I'm going to quit."

I said the words quietly, to no one in particular. I thought about my venting the night before. Quitting was the only thing that made sense. It hurt to open my eyes. It hurt to move. My body craved sleep with every muscle, joint, tendon, and molecule.

"Then you will never know the answer," insisted the same internal voice from a few hours prior.

"I've done my best."

I let myself slip back into unconsciousness, determined to sleep my fill before walking the two miles down to Route 56. It was a holiday weekend. There would be plenty of traffic. I didn't know what town I'd end up in, but it was Virginia—there were busses to everywhere.

"No, you haven't."

I opened my eyes, straining to discern whether they were indeed open in the inky blackness.

"You haven't done your best. You can still get up and you can still hike."

The voice was clear and commanding. Deep inside me there was an Anish who had not yet been vanquished. One still brimming with hope and fervor. I groaned as I rolled up to a sitting position and mechanically began to pack. Soon—just like every morning—I was walking by headlamp.

My movements were ponderous. After a couple of miles, I crossed a span bridge over Cripple Creek and reached the highway. The trail on the other side would have ordinarily beckoned me to follow it. But this time, my feet dragged across the tarmac, and even the squish of soft earth beneath the soles of my shoes when I reached the other side did nothing to cheer me up.

In the humid atmosphere, swimming seemed more appropriate than walking. An eerie sense of despair hung over the valley as I began to ascend The Priest. If time had been lost in a jumble before, it simply did not exist now. The pile of numerals on my internal clock had floated away into the fog. My body was disconnected from the part of me that willed it forward—the taskmaster that refused to let my feet stop. The miles dragged on slowly. *Why am I still here? Why am I still hiking? What is the answer?* I wandered through the wilderness, lost in my own mind.

I reached the upper crossing of Cripple Creek where it playfully bounded down the mountain. Even though the air was clammy by the water, I knelt down beside the stream. The dehydration of the day before layered sluggishness on top of my fatigue. I plunged my head into a small pool. The shock of the frigid water made me gasp.

I filled my water bladder and crossed the creek. Marching upward, I convulsed with cold and wished I were still asleep in my warm sleeping bag. When my hands turned blue I spiraled into self-pity and despair. As I climbed, the fog sank lower and lower until it engulfed me. The hushed woods were cool for the first time since the White Mountains. I shivered, regretting the dunking. *At least it's keeping me awake.*

I did nothing to check the tears oozing out of the corners of my eyes. *Why me? This is so hard. It's so unfair. This is harder than it should be. Why me?* I felt piteous. Weak. Deflated.

"I should have just quit at the highway," I told myself. "What's the point? I can't do this anymore. I can't go on." A shuddering sob accompanied my words.

I stubbed my toe and screamed, "This sucks!"

I blinked hard, forcing the pent-up tears lingering on my lower eyelids to make a decision. They succumbed to gravity and rolled down my red, numb cheeks. I thought about my mom. Her stroke was what was unfair. Out of nowhere her own body had turned on her. Her own brain had defied its role and threatened to kill her. She'd met the angel beyond the bright light and refused to follow. She'd come back unable to speak. Unable to write. To do much of anything. But she'd come back willing to work to regain those things that were lost. I blinked again. I could feel her presence near me—even though she was hundreds of miles away. I knew that every day I'd been walking she'd been in therapy. Fighting her own body. Relearning everything she'd once known how to do, unrelenting in her determination. I was not there to see it, but I could sense it. I could always perceive this woman of my blood and bone no matter how far apart we were. She was the most stubborn woman I knew. And, also, the strongest.

"You chose this, Anish. This was your choice. She didn't," I whispered sternly.

I stopped and wiped the tears off my face angrily. Staring up the trail, I traced its brown line until it disappeared into swirling mist. It was my own stubborn choice to battle my demons in the mountains, forty-some-odd miles at a time. There were plenty of people fighting battles they did not choose.

"Unfairness is part of life. This hike is not unfair. Quit if you want, but don't feel sorry for yourself," the voice of the unconquerable Anish admonished.

Give my mother strength. I resumed my climb heavenward. *Give my mother strength.* I repeated the prayer over and over in my mind as I ascended. The mantra left no room for self-pity. In response to this new mental intonation, my body relinquished its resistance. I was choosing to go forward. I was the progeny of tenacity and toughness and I would not martyr myself. I had chosen my own battlefield. *"I sure as hell had better fight."*

I grit my teeth together. "This trail is relentless," I said, and pushed off with my poles. "But then again, so am I."

Looming above in the misty stillness, The Priest presided over my transubstantiation.

RELENTLESS

VOICES FLOATED UP TO my ears from behind, softened by the dripping leaves and fog. *Runners.* I knew it had to be. They were the only ones who ever caught up to me. I surged forward, trying to delay the inevitable. Then I grimaced in amusement at my own hubris. *A few hours ago, you collapsed in a pile of rocks and lay there, intent on quitting. Now you're racing trail runners up The Priest?* As the voices and accompanying footfalls drew close, I stepped to the side of the trail without turning to talk to them. For days I'd been longing for someone to clear the spiderwebs and perhaps lessen my loneliness. But now that there were people on the trail, I wanted them to disappear so that I could sink deeper into myself.

"Hi!"

"Good morning!"

"OMG, Anish!"

Three ponytailed women dressed in tech tees and tiny shorts halted as the last in line recognized me.

"Hi," I responded.

"We were *just* talking about you! You're so incredible!"

"Thanks," I said, straining for a semblance of normal conversation. "Out for a run?"

"Yeah, every Labor Day weekend we run a section of the AT. We're the Dirty Mother Runners."

I smiled at the name.

"We don't want to hold you up!"

"It's ok," I said. "I think you're moving a bit faster."

"See you later!"

I followed them up the trail, but after a few minutes they vanished into the fog, their voices growing fainter until I was alone again. Finally, I reached the broad summit and turned off onto the blue-blazed trail leading to the Priest shelter. *Hopefully the spring has water.* I was surprised to see the runners snacking in front of the lean-to. They waved and cheered at my arrival. I returned the wave and set about filling my water from the trickling spring nearby.

"You're doing great!" one of them said. "We were wondering if we'd see you out here."

"Yeah, we are running all the way to Daleville," said another. "We'll probably see you several times this weekend."

"So how exactly are you doing this?" I asked, noting their minimal running packs.

"Oh, there's a fourth woman. You'll see her soon. She's running from the next road crossing south of here. She'll get back to Cripple Creek and one of us will have gotten the car from up ahead to go get her. We sort of leapfrog each other and the car."

"We don't camp," added one of the women.

They laughed.

"Yeah, we drink wine and sleep in a cozy cabin!"

"Sounds pretty awesome," I said.

"Well, I'm getting cold, we should go. We'll see you later today!"

"Thanks. Have fun!"

I ate a bar and headed down the mountain. Suddenly the travails of the day before were a faint memory. My head still ached from the lack of sleep, but I'd moved outside myself and my pain. As a bonus, I'd also found a connection with other female endurance athletes.

"Thank you," I whispered to no one and everything.

I noted the lack of spiderwebs and the ease of miles now that the enormous back-to-back climbs were done. I'd demanded something give—and it had. Inside my soul, the walls began to crumble.

"The trail provides," I said, smiling as I recited the mantra of hikers everywhere.

~

I crossed the partially open summit of Bluff Mountain as the first rays of light stained the horizon. Daily, there was an ebb and flow. Most mornings I was angry, tired, or resentful—all the negative emotions. I'd never been a morning person; I enjoyed sleep almost as much as I enjoyed hiking. Sleep deprivation was my biggest sacrifice for a record. However, once I made it through the first few hours—after the sun rose and sleep had fully receded from the corners of my eyes and mind—I began to enjoy the hike again.

I enjoyed the way my mind could wander while my body set itself to the repetitive task of thru-hiking. I enjoyed the cool breezes, mossy trees, and squirrel chatter. And I enjoyed the meditative quality of the journey—it was what I thrived on. I thought about my parents nonstop as I climbed and descended. I'd come so close to losing my mom two months ago. A memory from thirty years back, of the first time losing a parent had entered my mind, surfaced.

I had been out on the tractor with my dad, and he had slowed the machine to a crawl to tell me the forested acres of our home surrounding us would all be mine someday. Tears welled up in my eyes at the thought of my parents dying, and the world became a blurred mass of tree shapes and golden light. But I didn't cry. I nodded resolutely and said "ok" with all the solemnity I could muster.

Michigan, however, could only hold me for so long. I'd moved west as soon as I'd gotten the chance—right to the ocean's edge. Where mountains rippled and there were wild places yet unexplored. Every time I returned to Michigan I was greeted by an even patchwork of forest and field. Cities constructed from perfect grids of lights and pavement. The familiar flat land elicited a sense of happiness, safety, and homeland. As did the crumpled world below the plane when I returned to my Washington home—like wrapping paper five minutes after a Christmas frenzy. There, white cloaked the highest peaks, jewels of water glimmered from impossible perches. The aura of adventure seeping from those nooks and peaks enthralled me.

When my parents had come to Montana to see me off on the Continental Divide Trail in 2006, my mom saw the Rockies clearly for the first time. She told me later how she had realized their enormity—and the path I would be walking.

"When we flew out of Kalispell, I looked out the window and saw those mountains in every direction. And I thought to myself, my *baby* is going to walk over those."

I could imagine her—tears in her eyes, praying softly, face pressed to the tiny window—staring at the labyrinth of topography below. As the Continental Divide faded into the distance she would have sighed and leaned back against the seat—still praying.

My own eyes filled with tears thinking of her on that plane so many years ago. Where my mom saw hardship and danger, I saw beauty and freedom—my true happiness. The greatest moments of my life had taken place in the mountains. Every day I wasn't there, my heart ached to return—to the Rockies, the Appalachians, the Cascades, the Sierra Nevada. My heart beat for the mountains I'd walked through and for those I hadn't yet explored.

I wasn't sure how my all-consuming love for the highest peaks had happened, considering the land of my birth. Yet, the knowledge I would always have a home in Michigan had given me the fearlessness to embark on an adventure of exploration, and possibly fail. Like training wheels, my Michigan home provided stability for me to go and find myself—to fall in love with a foreign world of crags, precipices, and narrow dirt paths. I knew the time had come for the training wheels to come off. I was steadily carving my future with muddy shoes.

I was ten miles into my day—getting water at the spring in Johns Hollow—when the runners passed me again. We greeted one another before they carried onward while I finished filtering. I continued spiraling down the mountain toward the James River—one of the Appalachian Trail's lowest points at less than 700 feet above sea level. Soon I reached the 650-foot span over the cocoa-colored river.

Thud, thud. Thud, thud. Thud, thud.

My feet hit the bridge planking rhythmically and I felt the muscles in my legs tighten as I flew over the water. I turned right and glided down the trail as it undulated alongside the river. Just over forty hours ago I was debilitated, lying in the trail, certain I couldn't go on. Now, nearly halfway through Virginia, I felt the power of the James seep into me. Though I was a terrestrial, it was always the water—its power carried from the heavens to the mountains to the sea and back again—that reinvigorated me. I poured it into my body when I was thirsty. I waded in it—not always by choice. Other times, I followed alongside it, allowing the energy to course through me.

I reached Matts Creek shelter and looked up into the forest. The Appalachian Trail climbed 2,200 feet from there to Highcock Knob and beyond, spiraling up from one of the lowest points to the sky-skimming Blue Ridge Parkway. I took a breath, drawing the power deep into my belly. It was time to climb.

~

Reaching the Daleville Kroger beyond the Blue Ridge was an achievement in and of itself. I was completely out of food when I walked into the parking lot, despite the trail magic the runners had left at a road crossing for thru-hikers the day before. My hunger had surpassed symptomatic tummy growls and crankiness—for most of the day I'd been hiking in a woozy, light-headed state. The most direct path to reach the door of the supermarket passed by a Wendy's, and I couldn't last the extra hundred yards. I veered into the fast-food building and emerged minutes later with a large Frosty that was gone by the time I walked into the Kroger.

Revitalized by the sugar racing through my bloodstream, I made my purchases rapidly, including food to eat then and there. Outside I made myself at home at the picnic table the employees used for their smoke breaks. I chatted with them as they came and went while I ate and organized my new resupply—a full 3,500 calories per day to carry me the 119 miles to my box at Trent's Grocery, just off the trail in Bland, Virginia.

I looked down at the grimy, formerly white, floral dress I wore. It was fraying at the hem and I'd noticed the fabric on the back was nearly see-through. It stank. But despite its current condition, it still brought me joy. I remembered what it looked like under the dirt and the filth. I would be sad to see it go into the trash when I got my new dress at Trent's. My watch beeped, bringing me back to the present. It was time to go. Every bone in my body was like lead, weighing me down onto the bench. I picked up the bottle of caffeine pills I'd bought, bit one in half, and swallowed it with the last of my Coke. It was going to be a long night.

∼

Across Virginia, I moved all day and well into each night. Every day I pushed for the elusive fifty-mile mark. Yet, every day I fell a mile or two short.

It was a struggle to find enough water. Day after day, I added miles to my hike by taking the side trails to shelters that were usually located by reliable springs and streams. Which is how—several days later—I found myself at the Doc's Knob shelter crawling on hands and knees under rhododendron bushes, searching for water, at 4:45 a.m.

"C'mon," I whispered with frustration.

I could hear the burble of flowing water beneath the rocks. Finally, I located a gap in between the stones of the Devil's Racecourse big enough for me to wedge my bottle into. After an uncomfortable night without fluids, I was thankful to once again fill my belly with clear, cool water. I walked away from the shelter with more than I needed, content to carry the extra weight so as not to be thirsty again.

I reached rural Route 606 and turned right. A quarter mile later, Trent's Grocery came into view. It was a convenience store, but thankfully it held hiker boxes and—perhaps equally important—offered showers. I entered the tiny store and asked for my box. As the woman returned from the back room with it, I felt extreme relief at the sight of the familiar Priority Mail Flat Rate box, covered in pink zebra-print tape and Strawberry Shortcake stickers.

"Can I buy a shower?"

"Sure, it's three dollars. Go down the gravel drive behind here and there's a cinder-block building on your right. Soap is in there."

"Thanks."

I followed her instructions to a meager building that didn't have a functioning light. It also appeared that no one had cleaned it yet this hiking season. The door lacked both a knob and a lock. But there was a rock sitting on the floor inside—apparently to hold the shower door open or closed. I briefly considered its life prior to its role as a doorkeeper. The stone was smooth, indicating it had lived in a river before it was brought to the rundown shower room behind Trent's.

"We're both a little out of place, huh?"

I pushed the rock into the doorway so the door was propped open slightly, letting in the sunlight from the warm Virginia day. With enough light to see, I hung my pack on the hook and got into the shower. I refused to shower with my headlamp on. Since I'd already dumped the contents of my resupply into my pack, I set the empty box on the floor and threw a ravaged pair of socks along with my dress into it. I started to kick off my shoes, then glanced at the dirty shower floor and reconsidered. Instead, I carefully removed the socks I was wearing—the ones that would continue down the trail with me—and stuffed my feet back into my beat-up shoes before stepping into the scalding spray.

I stood there for a long time, letting the water power wash the dirt and sweat from nearly seven hundred miles off of my body. I looked for shampoo and soap only to discover that the sole cleanser in the entire bathhouse was a bottle of Palmolive. Reluctantly, I squirted the green goo into my hands and washed my body. I thought about using it on my hair, but decided to simply rinse and scrub my scalp with water alone. *At least the soap is an excellent detergent for my socks.*

I dried off with the trashed dress and slipped on my new one. It sent a tiny quiver of happiness through me, making it easier to part with my faithful frock. The new dress was green with miniature pink flowers, one I'd sewn for myself years before. I'd worn it on the PCT from White Pass to the Canadian border in 2013, when I'd set an FKT. I hoped it would be a talisman of success yet again.

Shuffling out into the sunshine, I stepped out of my soggy, worn-out shoes and onto the grass. I wiggled my feet into new, dry socks and shoes. Despite the dish soap, which was already making my skin itch, I felt like a whole new woman. One with 610 miles to walk before she could really, truly rest.

～

I made my way over the rolling hillsides and crossed checkerboards of pasture and copse. I bridged endless fence lines on wooden stiles. The tiny ladders wore me down with their three step ups and three step downs after so many miles. I dreaded them each time I left the woods and walked through the grasslands.

The world revolved yet again into inky blackness as I dragged my unwilling body up the slopes of Walker Mountain. At this point, I craved sleep more than I craved food. I also craved the sense of progress that accompanied crossing a state line. *I need to get out of Virginia. Only a hundred more miles.*

The trail finally flattened as it bypassed the summit and continued along a ridge. A sound up ahead got the attention of my weary brain: crossing the trail in front of me—eyes glinting in my headlamp—was a mountain lion.

"Hey!"

By the time I could focus my eyes, I was alone, yelling into the dark. *Did I just see that?* I strained my ears to listen. The muted sound of an animal moving away, downhill, floated back to me. It was not fleeing. The only noise was a hushed saunter. I shook my head, feeling delirious with fatigue. *I didn't even know there were mountain lions in Virginia—probably a bobcat.*

Wobbling, I continued down the trail. I was not frightened by my encounter. My only thought was of sleep—and water. I found a streamlet and knelt down beside it, filtering water in the peaceful silence of the night. After so many nights on trail, I'd grown accustomed to the forest at the witching hour. I needed to sleep more, but three or four hours sufficed. *It will be over soon. Just keep doing your best.* I found a campsite and pitched my tent. At some point over the next few hours it began to rain. I woke to the relentless pounding on my tent. It was also brutally cold, when just a few days ago I had been dying from the heat.

"Oh God...." I murmured, squeezing caffeinated Trail Butter into my mouth.

I shivered as I packed up and donned my rain jacket. I was poncho-less for the next few miles, until I picked up my box from The Barn Restaurant at the highway crossing. The leafy boughs provided a reprieve from the full assault of the rain, but when I reached my first stile and pasture of the day, it was obvious I was going to get thoroughly soaked. I rushed through the wet grass and wide-open fields, cringing as water poured down my bare legs and into my shoes. At the highway, I half jogged toward the big red barn across I-81.

I sat down at a booth in The Barn Restaurant and perused the menu while rain pummeled the windows. I was happy to be inside, even though I was soaked.

A server came out from the kitchen and crossed over to my table. "What can I get you?"

"Coffee."

She poured me a cup of coffee thin enough to read a newspaper through.

"Uhm, and an omelet with everything in it. And sausage."

She disappeared for barely two minutes, during which I gulped down the dishwater coffee. She set the plate of food in front of me.

"More coffee?"

"Yes."

She poured me another cup and I began shoveling food into my mouth. There were advantages to being the only customer on a wet morning. She circulated past again.

"Can I have some more coffee?"

After I finished the third cup, I waved her over for more. She rolled her eyes and filled it.

"You can just leave the carafe if you want," I said.

"I'll come back."

I dug into my pack and pulled out a Starbucks VIA packet. I emptied half of it into the cup and stirred. After repeating this with my fifth cup of coffee I finally felt the effects of the caffeine blossoming in my weary mind.

"Can I also get my box?" I asked the server.

She brought it out and I quickly dug through it, putting the new food into my backpack. I opened the new poncho thankfully—it was still pouring rain. I tucked a generous tip under my plate and went to the front desk, where a new waitress was standing. I could see the first woman in the kitchen.

"Hi, can I possibly get a large coffee to go, please?"

"Sure thing, hon."

Gripping my coffee, I walked out into the rain and headed down the street. At the gas station, I bought a pair of rubber gloves and some hand warmers. I was going to need them to get through the sudden onslaught of autumn.

~

I crossed Grayson Highlands State Park on a sunny day surprisingly devoid of people. Feral ponies grazed in the rolling meadows and the crisp air smelled of the changing season. A stone's throw from Mount Rogers—the highest point in Virginia—I stopped briefly to take in the vista of rounded hills tinted with the mellow golden tones of late afternoon.

Inexplicably, I was drawn here, to the Appalachians. To their sustained ridgelines and rolling summits. There was always a quiet whisper of home whenever my feet touched their ancient rocks. I wondered idly if the reason lay in their geologic history and the fact that my family was firmly rooted in Scotland. The Scottish Highlands and the Appalachians were the same mountain range, divided by millennia of continental drift. Once known as the Central Pangean Mountains, their dispersed remnants lingered on either side of the Atlantic. When the Highlanders left their homeland, they came en masse here: to the southern Appalachians. I closed my eyes and felt the wind gently lift wispy ringlets of sweaty hair away from my face. I listened closely—as I often did on silent mornings and starless nights. In the stillness, I could swear I heard the mountains murmur of those days gone by—when they soared above the world and clasped hands where oceans now lie. I smiled and unrooted my feet slowly from where they connected me to the earth.

"Home sweet home," I whispered.

~

I hunkered down to sleep ten miles from Damascus, Virginia. The town is known for its Trail Days festivities every spring. It was where I'd finally pared down my gear and started logging twenty-five to thirty miles per day northward on my first AT thru-hike. It was also where I'd met my ex-husband a year later on his first thru-hike. The Appalachian Trail passed through the town and, by and large, the community embraced the transient masses that traveled it.

I woke up shivering without the aid of my alarm at 3:45 a.m. There was no chance of falling back asleep so I got out of my tent and packed up. A heavy frost hung on everything. I didn't bother taking my pajamas off, and instead put my dress on over them before donning my hat and gloves. Then I wrapped my sleeping bag around my shoulders, tucking the foot and head of the bag into the neckline of my rain jacket. Finally, I zipped the puff into place and put on my pack.

I strode into Damascus at seven, affected by the mix of emotions stemming from my arrival in a pivotal place from my past. The town was different now. Most noticeable was a coffee shop, literally on the AT at the north end of town, open for early birds. I was thrilled to thaw inside a heated building while holding a steaming Americano. After I'd devoured the two kinds of gluten-free pastries they sold, the barista came over and set two deliciously ripe peaches on my table.

"Thought you might like these," she said, smiling.

"Thank you so much!" I picked one up and bit into it.

I nearly cried with gratitude and pleasure. The peaches were delicious and her kindness reminded me that seeing goodness and generosity in the hearts of others was one of the most notable gifts of thru-hiking.

Mount Rogers Outfitters, where my resupply box was waiting, did not open until nine. I knew if I bought food at the dollar store across the street instead of waiting, I would be back on the trail before then. But I wanted to relish this time to charge my phone and rest. I bought two more pastries and ate them slowly—savoring the flavors the second time around.

Finally, it was time to collect my resupply box. I repacked while chatting with the proprietor and, less than an hour later, followed the white-blazed sidewalks out to the edge of Damascus where the AT climbed up into the forest. I looked up at the ridgeline and thought of my descent into town in June 2003. I remembered how—far above the street where I now stood—I'd smelled the sweet scent of cut grass and headiness of flowering plants. I could vividly remember the deafening buzz of cicadas filling the trees, their sound nearly overwhelming that of the lawn mowers. It was the moment spring ended and summer began. I recalled the pangs of homesickness that had stabbed me in the gut. Homesickness for summer Saturdays when my dad woke me up by revving the lawn mower promptly at 9 a.m. Homesickness for cookouts on the deck where he charred the venison black—but we ate it anyway without a word of complaint along with the hot, buttery corn on the cob from our garden.

I missed building things with my mom in her toolshed—learning how to measure twice and cut once with power saws, tape measures, and squares. I smiled, thinking of my sixteenth birthday gift from her: my very own toolbox full of everything I needed for basic carpentry—and the note telling me to hide them from my dad. Building was our hobby and our laugh-be-hind-the-scenes secret. My father never did find where my mom's tools were—she hid them so he wouldn't break them by using them inappropriately. And I never got tired of her knowledge shocking the clerks at Sears when she went in to pick out new power tools. I was surprised that those memories were strong even now, so many years later. I realized it was because I was still homesick for my parents and our summers together.

As I was about to leave pavement for trail tread, a man on a bike caught up to me. I paused to greet him and he apologized for stopping me.

"I don't want to keep you. I know you have a long way to go today."

I assured him I didn't mind, and we talked for a minute or two.

He sent me on my way with a benediction, "May your feet be sure, your heart full of wonder, and may you go with God."

"Thank you. So much."

There was not much else I could say. I turned and began to climb up the mountain, glancing back to see him pedaling away.

"News travels fast in a trail town," I murmured. The wilderness was quiet and smelled of warm, damp autumn. No lawn mowers roared. No cicadas chirped. I missed my parents more than I had in 2003. I missed how healthy they used to be. I knew that if I had the chance now, I could win a race, hit a baseball, or fly a kite for my dad. I knew that if she wasn't relearning how to walk, write, talk—live—that my mom and I could be building cabinets or quilting, or taking impromptu roadtrips. Yet, I also knew the past was not where I lived. *I live here in these mountains now—finding myself yet again, becoming Anish more fully than when I was twenty-one.*

Nostalgia, excitement, and more muddled emotions I couldn't quite discern overwhelmed me as I hiked. It was only a few miles to Tennessee. Over and over, I recited the beautiful blessing spoken by the man on the bicycle. I knew I would continue to do so over the last week and final miles of the hike. For the first time in many days, I felt that my feet were indeed sure, my heart was incredibly full of wonder, and that God was ever present. The trail was my sanctuary, more so now than ever before. It was the only place I could feel whole, content, and connected to all that was beyond myself.

THE BEAUTY SPOT

I'D REACHED THE SISYPHEAN state. My life as it had been merely two months ago was now nothing more than a vivid dream only vaguely remembered. For as long as I could clearly recall—and for the interminable future—my reality had been nothing but endless walking. Every day was the same: walking, walking for seventeen or eighteen hours a day. Sometimes I'd walk for twenty or more. I'd walk until my legs inevitably quivered with fatigue—only then could I stop.

The only interruption to the cycle was my watch's periodic beep, reminding me to eat just enough calories to carry me another hour. Having burned through my body's reserves, I could only go as far as the calories I ingested could fuel me. Somehow 4,000 a day were enough to spur me forward, but barely. My stomach roared at me round the clock.

This was the almost-end. The time when the glimmer of light at the end of the long, green tunnel never seemed to grow any brighter, even though the miles remaining dwindled steadily in chunks of forty-five.

I climbed and descended, over and over. The number of miles of the Appalachian Trail wholly contained in Tennessee were few.

Soon, on my protracted ascent up to the Roan Highlands, I would cross into North Carolina. From there many more miles wove along the border between these two states—a border formed by the twisted backbone of the ancient range.

As darkness descended, I put on my headlamp and began to climb toward North Carolina. I felt an irrational drive to go until I crossed the state line. *I need to feel progress. I need to hike fifty miles. I need to cross the border.* Nine o'clock came and went. So did ten. I didn't even try to staunch the exhausted tears oozing out of my eyes. I refused to stop until I reached North Carolina at Doll Flats—forty-nine miles from where I'd woken up. Once again, I would not reach the fifty-mile mark.

"What the hell is wrong with you, Anish? Why can't you even do fifty miles?" I berated myself out loud as I hiked.

I had no idea where I was in relation to Matt's record anymore. I only knew I was ahead of Liz Thomas's female self-supported record of eighty days. My relationship with the record had evolved, though. Now, it existed merely as a catalyst to keep me digging even more deeply into myself than I ever had before. My body was crumbling as I pushed it to the brink of sleep deprivation while demanding it perform. Even so, it was never enough to meet my ruthless expectations. I felt weak—useless. Yet, somewhere in my psyche I was certain that this juxtaposition was exactly what I needed. Driving my body to its breaking point—a process that had started on The Priest—was loosening something inside my soul. By reaching my utmost limit, I would heal myself. The call of the white blazes in my dream did not ensure success—they promised answers. I slowly spiraled up the switchbacks in the pitch-dark, resolutely balanced on a sliver of rocky tread and my own fragility.

~

I woke up to moonlight illuminating my tent and cold fog rolling around the meadows. I silenced my alarm and was walking within minutes. After a meager three hours yet again, my joints and muscles felt gelatinous and slow. I crossed bare Hump Mountain as first light tinged the eastern horizon orange—revealing the rounded silhouettes of the Appalachian range as it emerged from dusky lavender. To the west, the world remained cloaked in navy darkness—a few stars still glimmering. I stopped, my body sighting due south, down the ridgeline.

My ancestors believed there were times and places where the physical and spiritual worlds came together. In the modern day, I'd often found these thin places—such as Crater Lake, Oregon— in the mountains, and there felt as though I too could glimpse what lay behind the curtain separating these worlds. They also believed in the time between times, the moment when night and day diverged—or when an eclipse married the two.

On the grassy slopes of Hump Mountain that morning, I straddled the time between times. Day skimmed my left side while night still clung to my right. The vastness, joy, and heart-aching beauty of creation throbbed in every cell of my body and soul—as it did in the presence of both birth and death. I took a deep, shuddering breath and wiped my eyes.

"May your feet be sure, your heart full of wonder, and may you go with God."

It lasted but a few seconds. Then the curtain wavered in the breeze that always accompanies dawn. Molten gold spilled over the rim of the world, bathing me in its glow. Night fled westward, wrapping the lingering stars in her cloak and vanishing beyond the mountains. Eventually the wonder rooting me in place dissipated and I headed downhill.

Thousands of feet of gain and loss over many balds—the treeless summits scattered across the southern Appalachians— marked my ascent to Roan High Knob. The glorious sunrise had given way to leaden clouds and arctic wind by the time I reached the 6,200-foot mountain, fourteen miles from where I'd slept.

I shivered in my sundress and kept stubbing my frozen toes on roots, cursing with pain every time. Finally, in the spruce forest near the summit, I stopped to don my paltry layers. Most of my body fat had already been sacrificed to the rocks, mud, and miles of the Appalachian Trail, so there wasn't much left to keep me warm as the weather transitioned resolutely toward the equinox. A few days before I'd been suffering in the heat and humidity of a mid-Atlantic summer. Now, I was shivering in my shoes. I wondered if I'd be able to keep warm crossing the Great Smoky Mountains—the highest part of the entire trail.

Hours later I reached the Cherry Gap shelter where it sat nestled among rhododendrons alongside a stream. It was unoccupied even though only an hour of daylight remained. I stopped briefly and glanced around the inviting glade. Smiling slightly, I recalled my first time there.

Darkness had begun to descend as I'd crossed the top of Unaka Mountain. I had no light and no idea how far the next shelter was. In fact, without any guidebook, I hadn't even known the mountain was there. Eerie mist began to wind its way through the whispering spruces and I'd fled—terrified—running pell-mell with my pack smacking me in the back. I'd tripped and fallen multiple times, tears streaking down my face. I had been so scared to be in the woods—alone—after dark. Night had just finished overtaking the day when I'd arrived at the Cherry Gap shelter with bloodied knees and palms, hyperventilating from my sobbing run. Finally safe, I'd wedged my mat down alongside several others who were already tucked in, cradling their pots of warm noodles.

"Looks like I'll be crossing Unaka in evening yet again," I said aloud. Turning away from the memories and empty shelter, I began my ascent toward a sacred mountain of the Cherokee.

I was no longer afraid of the long-gone voices I might hear rustling in the spruces. I was no longer a twenty-one-year-old neophyte who was afraid of the dark. I was Anish. I was at home out here, at any hour.

Unaka did not disappoint. I reached the enchanted conifer groves as mist rolled in around the trunks. The trees swayed and spoke softly among themselves. The time between times came and went as I moved through a place that had once terrified me. Tonight I simply acknowledged the sacredness residing there.

"Thank you, guardian mountain. I am passing through."

I stepped into my headlamp's headband like a pair of pants and pulled it up, situating the encased bulb at my waist. I turned it on low to complement the moonbeams piercing the thick canopy. Together they lit my way, undulating patterns of luminescence interspersed by the dancing shadows of the boughs above. Watching my own silhouette weave in and out with those of the trees on this lonely night, I felt my ancestors come to me, a comfort in the sacred darkness.

We walked together, their shade mingling with mine, and I felt a warmth fill me. I was not alone. As we walked together in silence over the mountain, I could sense their approval—ghosts walking in the moonlight.

Miles later—near midnight—I crossed a dirt road and walked through a wooden gate, climbing to the grassy bald of Beauty Spot. Alone again under the nearly full moon, I turned off my headlamp and walked by moonlight across the open grass. The end was near and yet so far. *I'm exhausted.* My heart and soul longed to cover fifty miles each day and yet my body said no. *Are two multi-thousand-mile FKTs in three years too many? Will I fail so close to my goal? Am I even meeting my goal?* I didn't know how many days I'd been out anymore. There simply wasn't enough brainpower left to do math.

"Just a few more miles," I encouraged my weary body.

And what would happen to my body when I was done? I knew from my studies that the human body was capable of incredible physical feats when fueled by fight or flight—survival instinct. I'd placed myself into this state through duplicity. By pushing my body relentlessly, I'd tricked it into believing we had been fleeing a fatal predator for over two thousand miles. And I'd done that twice—first on the PCT, and now here. Forcing it through starvation and the depletion of my adrenal glands. Giving it the bare minimum of sleep and demanding it heal from its injuries without the time and resources to do so. In search of the truth about my athleticism—my self-worth—would I completely destroy my body?

My shadow stretched lithely in front of me and I watched it perfectly mirror my body. Squared shoulders, legs scissoring smoothly. My arms swinging trekking poles in precise synchronicity. Though I felt nothing but weakness and frustration, my shadow revealed something else entirely: raw power. I stopped in my tracks, startled at the beauty of it. My shadow halted as well, and stood before me, emanating wordless moxie. I looked down at my knees, feet, and legs—overwhelmed by the many places they had taken me, over so many mountains, through rivers and dry canyons, into deep snow, and across jagged lava flows. I'd hurt them, healed them, pushed them . . . and yet they had always rallied. I felt awash with the blessing of having done what I'd done and to still be driving forward into new realms of self-exploration.

I let go of the trekking poles, and watched them fall to the grass in perfect sync with their shadows. Then, I watched my shadow arms slowly wrap themselves around my body, squeezing tightly. I held myself in an embrace for several moments, silently thanking my body for everything it had done and would do. Tears ran down my cheeks—not because of difficulty, frustration, or pain this time—but because of deep, abiding joy.

"I love you," I whispered to myself for the very first time.

"I love you," I said again, louder, although my voice wavered. For the first time, I loved my body for all it was and wasn't—for all it had done and could do. I knew they were the first words of the answer I'd embarked on this journey to find. The rest surely lay somewhere in the miles ahead. I bent down and picked up my poles, resuming rangy strides across the mountaintop. My soul had broken loose from its tether to finally embrace my body. I felt whole—connected to myself, the mountains, and my ancestors, as well as to the universe, the heavens, and God. I would reach Georgia. Anish would stand on Springer Mountain again.

~

The daylight following a full moon always seems warmer, softer. It vies for your love, lest you forsake it for the placid, blue ambiance of the night. I climbed steadily in its warm glow through leaves tinged terra-cotta. Autumn was burgeoning in the southern Appalachians. I thought about my sixth-grade gym class, where—sweating profusely in the thick sweatpants I wore to hide my unshaven legs from the taunts of classmates—I'd vacillated between participation and apathy, all the while resenting my mom. "You're not old enough," she said when she had refused to let me shave, disavowing my development.

I thought about screaming into the night as I set the PCT FKT at the border of the US and Canada, a woman gone feral. By accepting herself she'd unleashed something untamable. I thought about the plunge off of Baxter Peak less than two months before—that step into an abyss of knowing what would come, and yet not certain what would come with it. I thought about lying like a broken marionette in a pile of rocks on the slopes of Three Ridges—followed by my screaming demands to the universe. I thought about the moment just a day prior when I'd called my own body worthless because it refused to carry me beyond mile forty-nine—because it could not cover fifty miles a day on less than five hours of sleep. I realized that I'd been at war with and lost inside my own body my entire life.

I tripped and fell. Getting up, I wiped the dirt from my knees. I could not even count the number of times my tired feet had caught themselves on the roots or rocks since I'd descended Katahdin. Over and over, I'd wished the Appalachian Trail had been easier—or that my body was more capable. Yet, it was the mud, rocks, and blazes of the AT that I'd needed to become steadfast—to shatter my disconnect—and finally realize the strength of my own flesh. Bright sunlight poured through the canopy of leaves as I took root inside my own body. I crested the climb of No Business Knob and walked past the shelter. No longer was I considering coasting the remaining 338 miles, content with the minimum output needed to break the women's record only. I would no longer rail against my body for its weaknesses. I was all-in—both for the hike and for life beyond the trail.

The woods smelled of damp earth, wild boar, and fall. The seasons were changing, as was I. My world sparkled with newfound contentedness and my feet were light, despite the heavy physical lassitude that consumed me. Roots and rocks that had once been impediments were now familiar instruments of maturation. Climbs that were foes were now allies. Here in the southern Appalachians, I felt the hourglass flip over as I drew closer to where Anish was born—confronting the mountains that had once challenged, enthralled, and created her—a woman with new perspectives of power and intimacy. If there was a way to return to the womb, I was doing so now. Winding my way ever southward, I was also going backward, toward Carter Gap shelter where I first signed my name as Anish. And from there, even farther to Springer Mountain the place where, one sunny day in May of 2003, Heather Anderson walked into the Appalachian Mountains—and never walked out.

When Anish had placed the pebble she'd carried from Georgia on the summit cairn of Mount Katahdin in 2003, it was also a headstone for the woman who'd started the journey 2,172 miles before.

"I didn't mean to abandon you," I whispered to myself.

For so long I had perceived this death and rebirth as a conquering strength. Then, last night under the moon, I'd moved from self-acceptance to self-love. With the shattering enormity of that paradigm shift had come the realization that, although I had grown strong and independent as Anish, it had come at the cost of self-abandonment. I'd left Heather on this trail—locking her away along with all my hurts and insecurities—leaving the wounds to fester and living a life only half-true to myself. Now, I'd found a sense of wholeness. Now, with all my broken pieces spilled out under the dazzling sunlight, I could finally heal. As I walked, I picked them up, one by one.

The war inside me was over.

17 SOARING

AS I CLIMBED BIG BALD, I noticed a canopy tent, table, and chairs set up on the trail ahead of me. Intrigued, I put my head down and focused on grinding upward until I reached them. When I got closer, I saw a woman seated behind the table, which was lined with small brown paper bags. Something told me they were not trail magic sack lunches.

"Hello," I said.

"Hi," responded a man standing near the table. He opened his hand and a bird flew out.

I stared after it in surprise as the woman made notes on her clipboard.

"We're a bird research team," he said, smiling at my stunned look. "We're capturing, measuring, and banding birds."

"Oh. What kind of birds? What are you measuring?"

"Whatever we catch in our net," the woman replied with a laugh. "This morning we had a Cooper's hawk of all things!"

"But mostly songbirds," the man chimed in, picking up one of the paper bags. "This is a migration route."

"We measure body fat, wingspan, and a few other metrics," the woman added, pointing at some tools on the table. She nodded at the man.

"Would you like to release this one?" He held the bag out.

"Absolutely! More than anything." I paused and looked back and forth between them.

"I'll show you," he said.

He reached into the bag and pulled out the tiniest gray songbird I'd ever seen. He held it out and I tentatively reached for it. "Grip it with your fingers like this. Let the head and neck rest here." He demonstrated, slowly rolling his hand over so I could see how he held the bird. "This way they can't flail and hurt themselves."

Carefully, we transferred the bird from his hand to mine. I drew in a deep breath as I felt the rapid beat of its heart throbbing against my palm. The strong sticks of its legs and feet perched in the open space of my closed fist. Its feathers were soft and warm against my skin.

"Now when you release it, open your hand slowly. The bird may not fly right away. Just hold steady and wait."

I turned to face south along the AT, raising my hand to heart level. Slowly I loosened my grasp. Instantly I felt the power of flight ignite in my palm as the bird shot down the trail and disappeared, embracing its freedom to fly.

"Wow," I breathed.

The researchers smiled at me and waved goodbye. I followed the flight path, resuming my climb toward sunset swiftly, like a bird released from a cage. For many hours I felt the ghost of a tiny life tingling on my hand. I also felt ready to soar along whatever path my life would follow after this hike.

∿

The next day I ran most of the way to Hot Springs, North Carolina. I'd packed the Damascus box based on a pace of fifty miles per day; I'd averaged closer to forty-four. Thus, instead of three days, it had taken me four and a half. Even with the extra box of granola bars I'd bought in Damascus, it wasn't enough. I was out of food from ten in the morning onward.

"I can't miss this box," I chided myself as I labored up Big Firescald Knob midday.

I glanced at my watch. Bluff Mountain Outfitters, where my box was waiting, closed at five o'clock. I also needed to use their computer to print my camping permit for Great Smoky Mountains National Park. The trail was steep and the day was growing hotter as sunlight percolated through the trees.

I was dizzy with low blood sugar, heat, and dehydration by the time I began the plummeting descent from Lovers Leap toward the French Broad River.

"A couple more switchbacks, along the river for half a mile. Climb up the embankment and over the guardrail. Cross the river and the railroad tracks. Outfitter is on the left midway through town." I coached my fatigued legs through what I expected of them, surprised at how clear my memory from twelve years prior was.

I reached the bridge and glanced at my watch: 4 p.m. I let out a sigh of relief mixed with surprise and exhaustion. I wasn't sure how I'd managed to do thirty-eight miles in a little less than twelve hours, but I was thankful. As I crossed the railroad tracks, I noticed a large sign hanging on the Iron Horse Station: "Espresso. Ice Cream." *My two primary food groups.*

I made a beeline for it and walked out moments later with a large Americano and a large mocha milkshake.

"Next stop, Bluff Mountain Outfitters. Then, night hike 'til I drop."

I slurped down the last of the milkshake as I walked into the outfitters a block away. Soon after, with both permit and resupply box, I settled down on the narrow benches outside. A woman walked by, paused, turned around, and came back.

"I'm Barbara," she said. "I work at the visitor center down the street. Would you like to come in and sort through your things there?"

I stared at her, then at the explosion of gear and food around my pack, flustered by options.

"It's heated. And there's Wi-Fi," she added, as she went into the outfitters.

I looked at my mess strewn across the entirety of the bench and spilling over onto the sidewalk. I shoved everything back into my pack and the box, and jumped to my feet when she came back out a few moments later.

"Thank you. I think it will be easier there," I said. "I have a lot of sorting to do."

I followed her past the hardware store and into the diminutive visitor center. After she had given me the Wi-Fi password, I sat on a bench and plugged in my phone. I made a quick post to my Facebook page, then began sorting and repacking the food and warmer layers I'd sent myself. My stomach growled—apparently it had already burned through the milkshake.

"Would you like an apple?" Barbara asked me, holding out a bright red fruit. "It's from a tree in my yard."

"Thank you!" I bit into it, delighting in its crisp sweetness.

As I restocked my food bag, I felt a thrill race through me. In six days I would be on Springer Mountain. Only one more box to collect—three and a half days ahead—at the Nantahala Outdoor Center (NOC).

"Are you posting a blog?"

I glanced up, startled from my ruminations. "No, but I have a Facebook page: Anish Hikes."

Barbara started skimming my Facebook page on her computer. I could see her face grow more and more contemplative as she scrolled. I finished my coffee and stuffed the new waterproof gloves and warmer hat from my box into the outer pocket of my pack.

"You are a powerful woman," Barbara said, looking up at me. "You have a story to share."

"I, uh. Well, thanks." I stood up, uncertain what to say in return.

Her gaze bore into me and I felt the same spiritual power that had come with the benediction I'd received a few days before on the streets of Damascus. Those words had carried me thus far. Barbara's words would carry me to the end.

"Safe journey, to the end of this trail and beyond," Barbara said.

"Thank you."

Fueled by caffeine and her blessing, the 3,000-foot climb up Bluff Mountain glided under my feet as though I were flying—skimming the earth. The southern Appalachians were the mountains of my past, and now my present. The ones I would hold in my heart for all the days of my life. I remembered how I'd been scared of a noise in the woods on this mountain in 2003. Looking back, it was likely a deer or even a squirrel. Yet, I'd been so terrified I'd broken my walking stick against a tree trying to make enough noise to scare the mystery animal away.

I laughed softly at myself as I rose up the mountain, my footsteps lit by moonlight and headlamps. The forest was replete with its sounds of life—sounds that no longer terrified me. Owls hooted back and forth to one another. Deer rustled in the brush as they bounded away. Trees waved—rubbing their boughs together with deep groans and loud squeals. I felt welcomed by the harmony and added my own rhythmic footfalls to the song.

~

As I traversed the seamless ridgelines of the Great Smoky Mountains, I thought about the parts of me that I'd locked away for over a decade. Why had I abandoned myself for so long?

Deep down I knew that though I gave my inner pain no conscious thought, it had been there with me all along. On every trail and mountaintop, calling for me to come to terms. Yet I had not answered, hiding and hoping, coping through stoicism. I contemplated the existence of a dark chamber inside everyone where they put the hurt, the embarrassments, the scars, the heartbreak—the pains of living—a place to lock them away and forget they exist in order to move on. It's how we cope and how we survive the harshness of an unfair world. Some people open the chamber when they're low and use the contents to berate themselves, reliving the rancor because they don't believe they deserve anything else. Some only open that chamber to throw more in and never process the pain. Now I was realizing I'd spent a lifetime doing both.

I'd discovered on the PCT that pushing myself to the physical and mental brink unlocked the chamber's door without my permission. Being at the brink made me raw and vulnerable—even when I was outwardly strong, courageous, and conquering. On the AT the chamber door stood open again, inviting me to pull out the sorrows and expose them to the light.

That chamber had been open for sixty days on the PCT, and I'd run from it. Over and over, I slammed it shut with my strength, stubbornness, and my courage to face every fear—except those within me. Now, the AT had laid me bare in ways the PCT hadn't. By pushing myself to my limit every day, there had been no reserve left to close the door to my soul. So, I'd begun to process and to cope—to look at the pain I'd carried for so long—until I emptied that chamber and found a way to love myself, flaws and all.

The small wooden sign marking the high point of the AT, on the flanks of Clingmans Dome at just over 6,600 feet, drew my attention back to the present.

"It's all downhill from here, or so they say," I muttered wryly, shaking my head to clear the deep thoughts that had been brooding.

I was essentially out of food yet again. No matter how much I carried, it would never be enough to quell my body's need for calories. I ploughed through 4,000 a day easily and still wanted more. Worse, it would be another race to reach the outfitter at the Nantahala Outdoor Center before they closed the following day. At least the extended ridgeline miles of the Smokies had passed quickly—most of what remained before I set up camp was the long final descent. My stomach growled and I glanced at my watch—still forty-five minutes until I could eat again.

A few miles later, as I cleared the upper switchback to Silers Bald, I heard a familiar scuffle in a tree to my left. I glanced toward it, only half-interested. I'd heard that noise frequently since northern Vermont. The trees were firmly rooted two switchbacks below, yet their upper branches stretched and soared—level with my line of sight. I noticed that the wind from the day before had begun the seasonal stripping of leaves, which made it easier to see the source of the noise I'd become so accustomed to: a lanky black bear perched on limbs that seemed inadequate to support its weight. The bear swayed gently with the crown of the tree, completely unaffected by the movement. It yanked the remaining leaves off of the branches and stuffed them in its mouth, along with whatever else *Ursus* eat while roosting in treetops.

"Oh my God!"

The bear glanced at me and went back to eating.

I rushed up the trail, thinking about how often I'd heard that exact sound over my head while night hiking. "And all this time I thought it was squirrels!"

Dusk came soon after, turning the woods completely black. I heard that same scuffling noise in the trees over and over. Now on heightened alert, I shone my headlamp in the direction of any suspicious sound. Over the next few hours I spotted half a dozen bears on the ground and heard at least that same number up in the trees.

"No wonder I've never seen a bear in the park," I said loudly. "They're only out at night!"

I crossed the woody saddle of Big Abrams Gap at ten. A bear with cubs fled from the light of my headlamp, back into the safety of darkness. I quickened my step, feeling as though I was watched.

"Only two miles to the shelter," I told myself, refusing to look over my shoulder or let myself be afraid.

The forest was now unnaturally silent, prickling the hair on the back of my neck and urging me forward. I took comfort in the knowledge that I'd soon be camping near people at Mollies Ridge shelter.

At last my headlamp beam caught the corner of the shelter. I hastened toward it, trying not to illuminate anyone sleeping there, while feeling unseen eyes follow my progress. I looked around for a spot to camp, and was surprised to see no other tents, even though it was a perfect fall evening. My instincts were screaming. Finally, I swung my light upward to quickly survey the interior of the wooden structure: it was absolutely empty.

"What the . . . ? Where is everyone?" I almost tripped over myself in my haste to retreat a few hundred feet to the seeming safety of the thread of trail.

There was something incredibly disconcerting about finding an empty shelter in the heavily visited Smokies. Hanging on the trail sign for the shelter—facing south—was a yellow park service sign. I walked over and turned north in order to read it.

"Warning: The next 3 miles are Heavy Bear Activity Areas. Exercise extreme caution."

Two seconds later I was moving south at top hiking speed.

"Really?! Where was the warning sign for me? What the hell, Smokies? What is this? Sacrifice the SoBos?"

My blood was pumping as I hiked farther from Mollies Ridge and closer to Fontana Dam. As the distance increased, the impression that I was being watched dissipated.

In the morning I moved quickly, losing elevation as I continued dropping from the highest part of the Appalachian Trail down to the Nantahala River at 1,600 feet, and the tallest dam in the eastern United States: Fontana Dam. Before sunrise had even considered arriving, I heard the unmistakable sound of claws on tree bark—ascending.

I paused, uncertain whether to hike on or wait. I could tell that the bear was in a tree not fifty feet ahead of me, right alongside the trail. A few seconds of silence reigned before I heard claws sliding down the bark. A thump, followed by thrashing through the brush downslope ensued. I took a few hesitant steps forward, thinking it was heading away from me. Then the sound came back toward me.

I halted. "Oh no!"

The crashing bear turned and paralleled the trail, heading southbound. I took a few more steps. Then the sound changed direction again and ran back toward me.

"For Pete's sake, just stop!" I exclaimed in frustration. "It's too early for this business."

The noise stopped and I hiked forward. At the base of the tree was a huge, steaming pile of bear scat.

"Sorry for scaring the shit out of you!" I yelled at the hidden bear, laughing.

I heard the bear barrel downhill through the brush and away as I hiked south.

The sky was gray and misting as I crossed Fontana Dam and walked toward the deserted visitor center. I circled the building, searching for trash cans and a water faucet. After finding them both by the bathrooms, I filled my water and tossed my garbage. Prepared to leave, something red caught my eye.

I walked over, thrilled to find a Coke machine.

"Hallelujah." I dug in my hip belt pocket for my wallet.

Despite the brisk morning I downed three ice-cold sodas in less than five minutes.

"Gotta get up Cheoah somehow," I muttered, shivering from all the chilled liquids in my body.

I jogged a bit as I continued through the dam complex on sidewalks, roads, and flat trail. By the time I passed the shelter a short distance away from the visitor center, I was warmed up and my body was responding to the rush of caffeine and sugar. I had to make it to the NOC outfitter—exactly thirty miles away—by 5 p.m. to pick up my box. There were what many thru-hikers frustratingly called pointless ups and downs—known as PUDs—followed by the steep ascent and descent of the 5,000-foot Cheoah Bald. It was shaping up to be a repeat of the day going into Hot Springs.

"It's time to fly," I urged my legs.

The gray morning had finally turned to broad daylight as I made my way toward Stecoah Gap—and prepared for the subsequent slog up Cheoah Bald. The bears had retired to their daytime hideaways and the diurnal species reigned once again. I spooked a rafter of wild turkeys, watching with glee as they gobbled and lobbed their immense weights into the air. Aloft, they cruised like tandem-rotor helicopters, cumbersome, yet swift. They landed on branches with the force of a body check into the boards at what they must have deemed a safe distance from me— shaking the entirety of the tree as they lighted. Their antics made me laugh aloud.

I ran whenever the trail was conducive and hiked as fast as I could the rest of the time. Unlike the trail into Hot Springs, these miles were steeper, and with more ups than downs. I had already blasted through my remaining food by the time I crossed the junction with Bartram Trail, a quarter mile from the summit of Cheoah Bald.

"Seven more miles," I coaxed myself, barely glancing at the expansive view of southern North Carolina, and perhaps even into Georgia. *I have two hours to get there.*

I was sweating profusely from the effort of moving so fast, encrusting my dress with salt. As I moved, vaulting over fallen logs and skipping down rocky switchbacks, the friction of the salt crystals in the fabric of my dress against my nearly empty pack rubbed sores into my back. Occasionally the trail would turn upward and I would curse in frustration. Even the slightest grade stole my ability to run. Yet as soon as it resumed a downward trajectory, I lengthened into a full-stride gallop once more.

"This is your last box, Anish. You never have to do this again. Just get it."

My legs threatened me with cramps as I urged them to go faster than they had for nearly two months. I was locked on to the objective. Following the trail down tightly coiled switchbacks, I caught a glimpse of the Nantahala River 500 feet below. Rocky outcrops jutted into the trail tread and I danced across them, praying no copperheads or rattlesnakes were basking there this afternoon. I crossed a railroad track that paralleled the river through the gorge and reached a large parking area. In front of me was an entire complex of buildings. My watch read 4:50 p.m.

"Which building?" I panicked.

I ran to the first one: it was locked. The second appeared to be a bathroom and changing room. Looking around, I spotted a couple of women by a footbridge and ran over to them.

"Hi, do you know where I can find the office?" I panted. "Or someone in charge? I need to pick up a box from the outfitter before they close."

One of the women pointed across the bridge. "Probably in there. That's the store and outfitter both, I think."

"Thank you!" I yelled over my shoulder as I sprinted across the Nantahala.

At the store, I grabbed the door handle and yanked, feeling relieved as it opened. I stumbled in and stood there panting for a moment. The clock on the wall read 4:57.

"You made it," a man with shoulder-length blond hair said, smiling.

"Do you have a box?" asked a woman who was sweeping the floor.

"Hi, yes. Yes, I did. I do. A box, yes. Heather Anderson." I blurted out a string of words that I hoped made sense. I was still dazed from the lack of calories and the all-out effort of the final miles.

"We're closing up here in a couple minutes, but take your time and get what you need," the blond man replied.

"Thank you."

I spun the impressively large rack of energy bars around and grabbed ten of varying brands and flavors. I knew what I needed—calories, lots of calories. The 4,000 a day I had been consuming simply weren't cutting it. The woman emerged from the back room with my box and I paid for my bars.

"Is it ok if I sit outside on the benches to go through this?"

"Absolutely."

I sat down under the awning and quickly ate the meal I'd included in my box. Then I peeled my worn-out socks off my feet and threw them in the trash can. I'd gotten new socks and shoes in Hot Springs and now, with only 136 miles left, I was confident I would make it to the end with one pair of socks. Next I swapped out my headlamp batteries, leaving the spent rechargeable battery pack on the bench. Every other nonessential item from my pack I culled—either throwing it away or adding it to my impromptu hiker box pile. I scrawled "free" on a flap of the box and set it beside the cast-off gear. At the still-open convenience store across the road, I bought some jerky, cheese, and another soda. I devoured it on the bench out front and then started up the trail.

It would be another long, late-night ascent to reach Wesser Bald, but my headlamp—juiced by the fresh batteries—was powerful. I relished the caress of the warm southern night on the bare skin of my arms and legs and the unusual treat of being a comfortable temperature while hiking. I lost track of time and effort as I watched the moths and assorted insects dance directly in front of my face—mesmerized by the beam of light emanating from my forehead. It was as though I sat in a theater beside the projector, watching a film about nocturnal life in the mountains.

To my surprise, a bat winged through the movie, voraciously scooping insects into its mouth. I understood completely. I too felt as though I could eat my bodyweight in food each day. Glancing down, I could see there wasn't much left of me at this point. Yet, the changes I had made in my diet since learning about my gluten intolerance, as well as overall improved nutrition, meant that even at this stage I felt stronger than I had on the PCT. I was thin, but I wasn't emaciated or consuming my own muscle tissue to survive.

The flutter of bat wings brought my attention back to the film. There were two now—dancing with one another as they devoured the insects inexorably drawn to the light. They swooped in and out of my headlamp's beam, darting with beautiful precision and rendering complex plot twists as we all floated upward together— in our silent nature film. One bat veered left into the forest as I ascended with the other for a few more yards. Finally, it swung toward me—soaring past my face in near silence. I felt the velvet softness of its leathery wing brush my bare shoulder and heard the muted whirr of disturbed air rush past my ear as it fluttered away.

Alone again, I relished the feeling of oneness with the wild night.

CARTER GAP

"HOW CAN I NOT FEEL STRONG as I push through the last miles of this journey?" I asked myself as I ascended Albert Mountain. My gait was powerful as I started the descent, picking my way down the mountain's vertiginous southern side with ease.

It's not often that someone can return to—or even recall—where they discovered their identity. But as I reached Carter Gap, watching the heated mist of my breath condense and rise before billowing around me, I knew I'd come back to that place at last. Rain drizzled through the rhododendrons arching overhead as I stood expectantly at the junction of the side trail, as if waiting for my own ghost. I closed my eyes and imagined my twenty-one-year-old self hobbling out of the shelter early in the morning, wearing stiff boots that were too small. Every morning my first steps were excruciating until the pain reached critical mass and my feet went numb in self-preservation—allowing me to walk until dark.

I remembered how the evening prior I'd sat barefoot on the floor, my bloody socks lying next to me. My heels, rubbed to raw hamburger, had bled nonstop for days. Desperate to alleviate some of the pain in my toes, I'd taken my scissors and attempted to trim my already short toenails even more. With one clip, a torrent of clear fluid had erupted from underneath my big toenail—and with it came a realization. After that I'd meticulously sterilized a needle with a lighter and plunged it into the giant blisters beneath every single toenail. As streams of fluid shot out, the excruciating pain of the previous week finally lessened.

Anish had been born that night—from fire and pain.

I remembered signing the register in the morning before I left. "Anish was here."

Now here I was, resurrecting Heather Anderson from the dark chamber. She had resided there alongside all her hurts, all her failings—perceived or otherwise. I had carried her from Beauty Spot back to where the ever-strong Anish had first left her—in the Carter Gap shelter. I touched the signpost at the junction, noting that the shelter I'd sat in was gone and a new one had been built on the opposite side of the trail.

"Right here." I breathed the words quietly while shivering—doused in memories as well as water.

The Appalachian Trail had given me the courage to empty that chamber. I had started with the small pains—embarrassing social interactions and the crashing of my She-Ra kite. Sometimes it was laughable that I'd allowed them to linger in my soul. Other times I grappled with them for days on end, remembering all the people who had told me that there was something wrong with me for being different. One by one I'd examined each and every injury residing there. It had taken all the strength and courage I had to hold them up to the light and carry them over rocks and roots, up mountains, and across rivers until they'd dissipated into the soft Appalachian nights. I'd pulled them out and refused to put them back until I could forgive and release—just like the tiny bird I'd held in my hand.

Through the process I discovered—to my absolute incredulity—that the deepest scars were not the ones inflicted by others. They were from the wounds I'd inflicted on myself. These cuts came each time I had told myself I failed. That I wasn't good enough. That I was ugly, fat, worthless, incapable. Tears had cascaded down my face as I healed those scars, proving them false with every forty-plus-mile day and every choice to continue, even when my goal seemed out of reach. The Pacific Crest Trail had prepared me, but it was the Appalachian Trail that finally cracked me open, allowing me to heal.

I stood face-to-face with The Ghost of myself, hobbling out of the shelter with a new name and a stubborn set to her jaw. Everyone in her life had told her she wasn't capable of walking to Maine. But for the first time, she had dared to believe they were wrong. The first weeks had been harder than she'd thought, but she refused to let them be right. For once in her life, she was going to be successful at something beyond academics.

I closed my eyes, noting the pungent scent of the rhododendron thicket. The equinox was tomorrow—summer's cloak was drawing shut. This circle of my life neared completion. I put my arms around the memory of Anish, and around myself, just as I had on Beauty Spot. I held on to her as though I would never let go. This journey from Katahdin had been a journey back in time to this very moment. I tasted the second half of the answer I sought on my tongue.

I opened my eyes, somewhat surprised not to see my younger self there in the fog. *What would I do if somehow I could talk to her here, as she walked away from the life she'd known into a new one?*

"It will be hard, Anish. So very hard. Every step of going your own path. But you are strong enough, Heather. You are *enough*. And it will be worth every sacrifice. Be brave. The best is yet to come." I whispered to Anish of the past, and also to my future self—one who would exist long after this hike was over. "You will make it."

I realized I was still embracing myself tightly, tears running down my face. Whether I set a record or not, I knew it was this moment—and the one on Beauty Spot—that mattered. The real answer as to why I was here, why I'd fought and struggled and triumphed for nearly two months, was to reunite Anish and Heather. To reconcile a loss that I hadn't even know I'd sustained when I began this journey. I loosened my grip, trusting the circle to stay clasped on its own. Then I wiped my eyes, and hiked into the growing darkness.

~

I saw something move out of the corner of my eye, startling me. Whipping my head around, I looked at where my backpack lay on the ground beside Muskrat Creek. A black-and-sand-colored animal was wriggling over my pack strap toward the edge of the water. The large salamander-like creature panicked at being caught in the beam of my headlamp and sped up until it flopped back into the water and disappeared. I finished filling my bottles, uncertain what I'd seen. Then I shouldered my pack and made my way along the last miles of North Carolina.

Daybreak's pearly light flooded Bly Gap as I descended toward the ancient, gnarled oak tree that reigned over the glade. I paused to touch its trunk and whisper a greeting before I swiftly hiked the final tenth of a mile to the border with Georgia.

"Last state. Seventy-eight miles to go," I said, letting out a deep exhalation. "It ends tomorrow."

The miles flew by as I ascended and descended the undulating terrain. The weather was perfect and the sunshine set the deciduous trees aglow in shades of amber and vert. Tomorrow I would stand on the mountain where it all began and bid it a final farewell. The day would come and go and I would not walk anymore until I decided to. I was on the cusp of a tomorrow I'd often felt would never arrive.

As I pushed into the duskiness for the last time, I felt the amelioration of walking with a sense of wholeness. The physical strain of my AT hike had exacted an almost incalculable toll over the past weeks, but the mental exertion had exceeded it. Now, I'd found tranquility after the strife. With a symphony of owls in seemingly every tree, as well as crickets and creatures whose names I did not know, I was surrounded by the orchestra of the night. I called back in soft hoots, trying to tell them how much I would miss their choruses. They responded from the blackness with assurances that we would sing together again.

SPRINGER MOUNTAIN

MY FINAL DAY ON the Appalachian Trail I woke up thirty-nine miles from Springer Mountain. The morning began like every other—mindlessly consuming calories, throwing my shoes on, and breaking camp. As I began walking, however, it became clear that this day would be different. I reached the hostel and small gear shop in Neel Gap before the store opened, and paused a moment in the breezeway. I'd planned to buy food for my final thirty-one miles there, but it was ridiculous to wait over an hour, so close to the end. I mentally calculated what was in my pack: a bag of goji berries, a chocolate bar, and some energy bites.

"It's enough," I said to myself. *You need nothing left after today.*

I crested the rocky summit of Blood Mountain as sunrise spilled across the southern Appalachians. In every direction, waves of humpbacked mountains crowned with gilded forests glowed as they joyously greeted the returning sun. I picked my way across the summit, down the rocks and past the stone shelter, feeling the surge of adrenaline that had been with me since I woke still flowing strong. I'd anticipated a late-evening arrival, but now I wondered if my body had other plans. At the end of the PCT, a similar wave had carried me the final two miles at a near sprint. *It can't last all day, can it?*

By eleven that morning, I'd relinquished myself to the surge, accepting it would indeed last until Springer. I charged forward, unable to stop; I couldn't slow down or pace myself, even through the hilly terrain. My body had decreed that the time for pacing was done and over. I flew toward Springer Mountain, pausing just long enough to send a text to the woman who was supposed to pick me up, asking her to arrive at six that evening instead of nine. She responded immediately that it was no problem.

I put my phone away and climbed up from Woody Gap. Now that I'd accepted it wasn't slowing down, I focused my attention, and love, on the way my body dove into its task with complete abandon. It was stronger than I'd thought possible. The feel of liquid energy flowing out of my adrenal glands was palpable—like molten fire and ice—flooding my veins and every tissue with power. I swam in the high, tasting everything and nothing at the same time.

Even as the golden wildwood became a blur, my vision sharpened almost painfully. I felt as though I could rip my contacts from my weak eyes and see 20/20. I could smell everything: my own sweat and the funk of my gear, boar piss and decomposing leaves, a mix of pine and tree bark, the detergent clinging to people I passed, fumes from the highway I roughly paralleled, the distinct scent of water flowing across the ground. I swore I could smell the sun itself as it filtered through the rhododendron canopy.

"I love you," I whispered to my body. It was transforming into the lioness I remembered from the PCT—or perhaps the cheetah I'd longed to become.

I burst out of the rhododendrons into a gravel parking lot, surprised to find it full of vehicles. I had covered thirty-eight miles in under thirteen hours. Weaving between them to the other side of the lot, I reached the singletrack trail marked with white blazes. "Springer Mountain .9"

I hurried past the sign, my eyes welling with tears. I gasped for dry breath.

"Anish, you can cry when you're done!" I admonished myself. The trail became rocky. *One last challenge from the Appalachian Trail.* I tripped repeatedly as I tried to rush. In that moment, there was nothing more important than getting to the top of the mountain. Minutes later, I lurched into a clearing where two women were standing, taking pictures of the view through the narrow gap in the trees.

"Is this the top?" I said, choking with desperation, adrenaline, and sobs. The voice hardly sounded like my own.

"Yes."

I took three more steps across the slabs to the boulder embedded with a bronze plaque that read "Southern Terminus of the Appalachian Trail." Collapsing onto it, I allowed myself to weep without reservation.

"Are you ok?" one of the women asked me.

I nodded, unable to speak. I slid down the front of the rock and put my head between my knees, continuing to bawl uncontrollably.

"Are you sure you're alright?"

I nodded again, gradually gaining composure as the emotion of nearly two months of pushing myself to the physical and mental limit flowed out of me onto Georgia soil.

Finally, I was able to carry on a conversation with the two women from Minnesota, but my attention remained divided. Eventually they left and I was able to pull my knees to my chest and stare out into the rolling blue mountains spreading beyond the summit. Letting out a deep belly exhalation, I picked up my phone and entered my hike's start and end times into an online calculator. I stared in disbelief at the answer it generated. I erased it and started again, but the result was the same.

Finally willing to accept the result, I contemplated the previous 54 days, 7 hours, and 48 minutes of my life. Near constant motion had carried me 2,189 miles from the summit of Mount

Katahdin in Maine to this very spot in the mountains of Georgia on a pleasant September evening. I thought about the hypothermic rain in the White Mountains and extreme humidity of the mid-Atlantic, the endless rocks and roots and mud, the chronic sleep deprivation, and how hungry I'd been—and still was. *Was it only two days ago that I stood outside the Carter Gap shelter in the rain, reminiscing about when I first signed my name as Anish there twelve years before?*

The exertion of living many lifetimes within a few weeks settled into my bones. Beyond that, I felt a sense of weightlessness as the crushing need to move toward a goal dissipated. *I am here. I did what I set out to do.* More so, I'd found the answers to all of my questions, even the ones I hadn't intended to explore. I picked up my phone again, and began to type.

> The trail has a way of answering the questions you most need answered, even if you are afraid to ask.
>
> Those that have followed me for a while know I've struggled with self-esteem my entire life. You would think setting the PCT speed record would change that.
>
> Yet it only gave the negative thoughts an even more insidious way to demoralize me, especially after I failed to set the JMT record last year.
>
> "The PCT was a fluke. You were simply the benefactor of lucky circumstances. You aren't athletic. You aren't able. You're a charlatan. You don't deserve to stand at the starting line of an ultra like Barkley."
>
> On and on the whispers go.
>
> I had to come here, to the AT, where my quest to find myself began 12 years ago and face those voices.
>
> I was afraid to ask, but the trail knew the question in my heart: "Was the PCT a fluke?"
>
> The AT answered with a resounding, "NO!"

I wrestled, not against the trail or external forces, but with them. If it were easy, the whispers of inadequacy would continue. Instead I was challenged every single minute.

In the dark hours when I was tired, lonely, and hungry, that is when the demons came. "Why didn't you stop with the PCT record? It will be your greatest achievement in life. You won't ever do anything else. Now you're out here and you're in over your head. You will fail. You can't do this. And everyone is going to know that you are nothing."

But, every footstep I took was a choice. A choice to face my own perceived inadequacies. Every footstep was a commitment. A commitment to deny that there was any truth to the words of the internal foes.

As the miles dwindled into the double digits, I became aware that I was crushing more than miles. I was crushing a lifetime of self-defeating beliefs.

So now, I walk off of Springer Mountain alone, just as I came. My pack, my feet, and my heart are light, unburdened at last.

And, I am aware that the end of every journey is simply the beginning of the next and that, far from being behind me, the greatest achievements of my life lie ahead.

New Appalachian Trail Overall Self-Supported Fastest Known Time: 54 days, 7 hours, 48 minutes.

~

I waited a few moments longer, savoring the private triumph before I birthed the story into the world. There the news would travel like wildfire—as soon as I left Springer Mountain I would be engulfed in it. I knew the trajectory that lay ahead and the role I would play in the coming media dance. But for now, I was still on a mountaintop, where I belonged.

"Thank you," I said softly to my feet.

"Thank you," I repeated to my legs.

I placed my hands on my heart.

"Thank you, most of all."

I posted the announcement, slowly stood, and began to retrace the rocky mile back to the parking lot. I dialed a number I knew by heart—one I'd called a thousand times—the oldest string of digits my memory held.

"Hello?"

"Hi, Mom, this is Heather. I'm done. I did it."

I clutched the phone tightly to my ear, wishing I could touch her. For several long seconds of silence, I held my breath.

"I'm so glad. I've been praying for you."

Her words were clear, even though she spoke slowly.

"You're talking so well, Mom," I said, my voice breaking.

She replied, "I've been working so hard in therapy, because I knew you were going through something so difficult too."

And we cried.

ACKNOWLEDGMENTS

THANK YOU TO THE Appalachian Trail Conservancy for your tireless work and dedication to maintaining a pristine footpath through the Wild East.

Thank you to my husband and biggest supporter, Adam. Without you, this itinerant author couldn't have made it work.

Thank you, Mom, for your endless prayers, unwavering support, and unconditional love. I would not be who I am without you and Dad.

And of course, thank you to Mountaineers Books and Kirsten Colton for continuing to work with a nomad who has a story to tell.

ABOUT THE AUTHOR

A National Geographic Adventurer of the Year, **Heather Anderson**, known as Anish on trails, became the first female Calendar Year Triple Crowner when she completed the Appalachian, Pacific Crest, and Continental Divide National Scenic Trails during one March to November season in 2018. This achievement made her the only female triple Triple Crowner, having completed all three trails three times. Anderson holds the overall self-supported, Fastest Known Time (FKT) on the PCT, hiking it in 60 days, 17 hours, 12 minutes, establishing the first female record and breaking the previous men's record by four days. She also holds the female, self-supported FKT on the AT, 54 days, 7 hours, 48 minutes, and the Arizona Trail, 19 days, 17 hours, 9 minutes.

In addition to hiking more than 40,000 miles since 2003, including fifteen thru-hikes, Anderson is a trail runner, avid mountaineer, and peakbagger working on several ascent lists in the US and abroad. She is also a professional speaker who shares her adventures and lessons learned on trail and the author of *Thirst: 2600 Miles to Home*, which chronicles her PCT record.

recreation • lifestyle • conservation

MOUNTAINEERS BOOKS, including its two imprints, Skipstone and Braided River, is a leading publisher of quality outdoor recreation, sustainability, and conservation titles. As a 501(c)(3) nonprofit, we are committed to supporting the environmental and educational goals of our organization by providing expert information on human-powered adventure, sustainable practices at home and on the trail, and preservation of wilderness.

Our publications are made possible through the generosity of donors, and through sales of 700 titles on outdoor recreation, sustainable lifestyle, and conservation. To donate, purchase books, or learn more, visit us online:

MOUNTAINEERS BOOKS

1001 SW Klickitat Way, Suite 201 • Seattle, WA 98134
800-553-4453 • mbooks@mountaineersbooks.org
www.mountaineersbooks.org

An independent nonprofit publisher since 1960

OTHER TITLES YOU MIGHT ENJOY FROM MOUNTAINEERS BOOKS

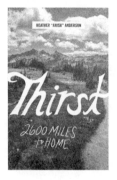

THIRST
2600 Miles to Home
Heather "Anish" Anderson

A memoir by the first
woman to hike the Triple
Crown in a calendar year

PEAK NUTRITION
Smart Fuel for
Outdoor Adventure
Maria Hines and
Mercedes Pollmeier

Simple, tasty recipes to
boost your motivation,
performance, and recovery

JOURNEYS NORTH
The Pacific Crest Trail
Barney Scout Mann

Mann, a legendary trail angel,
weaves together the stories
of six lives that become
intertwined as they hike from
Mexico to Canada

HIKER TRASH
Notes, Sketches, and
Other Detritus from
the Appalachian Trail
Sarah Kaizar

A curated collage representing
backpacking culture on the AT